Excel

Get the Results You Want!

Year 3 NAPLAN*-style Tests

**Associate Professor
James Athanasou
with Angella Deftereos**

PASCAL
PRESS

* This is not an officially endorsed publication of the NAPLAN program and is produced by Pascal Press independently of Australian governments.

© 2010 James Athanasou, Angella Deftereos and Pascal Press
Reprinted 2010 (twice)
Revised in 2011 for NAPLAN Test changes
New NAPLAN Test question formats added 2012
New NAPLAN Test question formats added 2013
Reprinted 2014, 2015
Conventions of Language questions updated 2016
Reprinted 2017, 2018

Revised in 2020 for the NAPLAN Online tests

Reprinted 2020, 2021, 2022, 2023, 2024

ISBN 978 1 74125 172 2

Pascal Press Pty Ltd
PO Box 250
Glebe NSW 2037
(02) 9198 1748
www.pascalpress.com.au

Publisher: Vivienne Joannou
Project editor: Mark Dixon
Edited by Tim Learner, Joanne Innes and Rosemary Peers
Proofread and answers checked by Peter Little and Dale Little
Cover and page design by DiZign Pty Ltd
Typeset by DiZign Pty Ltd, Kim Webber and Grizzly Graphics (Leanne Richters)
Printed by Vivar Printing/Green Giant Press

Reproduction and communication for educational purposes
The Australian *Copyright Act 1968* (the Act) allows a maximum of one chapter or 10% of this book, whichever is the greater, to be copied by any educational institution for its educational purposes provided that the educational institution (or the body that administers it) has given a remuneration notice to Copyright Agency under the Act.

For details of the Copyright Agency licence for educational institutions contact:

Copyright Agency
Level 12, 66 Goulburn Street
Sydney NSW 2000
Telephone: (02) 9394 7600
Facsimile: (02) 9394 7601
Email: memberservices@copyright.com.au

Reproduction and communication for other purposes
Except as permitted under the Act (for example, a fair dealing for the purposes of study, research, criticism or review) no part of this book may be reproduced, stored in a retrieval system, or transmitted in any form or by any means without prior written permission. All inquiries should be made to the publisher at the address above.
While care has been taken in the preparation of this study guide, students should check with their teachers about the exact requirements or content of the tests for which they are sitting.

NAPLAN is a trademark of the Australian Curriculum, Assessment and Reporting Authority (ACARA).

The publisher thanks the Royal Australian Mint for granting permission to use Australian currency coin designs in this book.

Notice of liability
The information contained in this book is distributed without warranty. While precautions have been taken in the preparation of this material, neither the authors nor Pascal Press shall have any liability to any person or entity with respect to any liability, loss or damage caused or alleged to be caused directly or indirectly by the instructions and content contained in the book.

All efforts have been made to gain permission for the copyright material reproduced in this book. In the event of any oversight, the publisher welcomes any information that will enable rectification of any reference or credit in subsequent editions.

INTRODUCTION

INTRODUCTION

Welcome to the *Excel Year 3 NAPLAN*-style Tests. This book has been specially written to help parents and teachers of Year 3 students in their preparation for the Year 3 NAPLAN Tests. It is also helpful as a general revision for Year 3.

This book was first published in 2010 and has been revised for NAPLAN changes several times. It has been widely used and many thousands of copies have been published throughout the years. In this edition the content has been reorganised for the new online version of the NAPLAN Tests.

The aim of this brief introduction is to provide parents, guardians and teachers with some background to NAPLAN.

The book is a collaboration by a specialist in educational testing and an experienced NAPLAN marker. Both are trained teachers.

It is designed for use by parents who want to help their son or daughter, and by teachers who wish to prepare their class for the NAPLAN tests. Some parents also use these books for general revision or when tutoring their son or daughter.

We hope that you will find this guide easy to use. In the following sections we will try to answer some frequently asked questions about the tests.

Associate Professor James Athanasou, LittB, MA, PhD, DipEd, MAPS
Angella Deftereos, BA, MTeach

What is different about this edition?

This is the latest and most thorough revision of the Year 3 book. It has been designed to accommodate the new online tests in an easy-to-use book format. The tests in this book contain excellent practice questions from very easy to very hard.

What is NAPLAN?

NAPLAN stands for *National Assessment Program—Literacy and Numeracy*. It is the largest educational testing program in Australia. It is conducted every year in March and the tests are taken by students in Year 3, Year 5, Year 7 and Year 9. All students in these year levels are expected to participate in the tests.

The tests cover Reading, Writing, Conventions of Language (Spelling, Grammar and Punctuation) and Numeracy. In other words, they cover what are known to many people as the basic skills of reading, writing and arithmetic.

What is the purpose of NAPLAN?

Although NAPLAN has been designed mainly to provide administrators and politicians with information about Australian schools and educational systems, it is also relevant for each pupil. It provides a public record of their educational achievement.

Increasingly it is among the most valuable series of tests students will undertake in their primary schooling and probably their first formal and public examination.

What is being assessed?

The content of NAPLAN is based on what is generally taught across Australia. So do not be surprised if NAPLAN does not match exactly what each child is learning in their class. Most schools should be teaching more than the basic levels.

NAPLAN covers only a specific range of skills. This is because literacy and numeracy are considered to be the basis of future learning in school. Of course we know that there are many other personal or social skills that are important in life.

We also realise that each child has their own special talents and aptitudes but at the same time governments also want to be able to assess their educational achievement in the fundamental skills. It is important to emphasise that there are many different kinds of literacy and numeracy, and that these tests cover only some aspects.

What is NAPLAN Online?

Until 2017 NAPLAN tests were all paper-and-pencil tests. From 2022 all students have taken the NAPLAN tests on a computer or on a tablet. With NAPLAN paper-and-pencil tests, all students in each year level took exactly the same tests. In the NAPLAN Online tests this isn't the case; instead, every student takes a tailor-made test based on their ability.

In the NAPLAN Online tests a student is given specially selected questions that try to match their ability. This means that in theory a very bright student should not have to waste time answering very easy questions. Similarly, in theory, a student who is not so capable should not be given difficult questions that are far too hard for them.

Please visit the official ACARA site for a detailed explanation of the tailored test process used in NAPLAN Online and also for general information about the tests: https://nap.edu.au/online-assessment.

These tailor-made tests will mean broadly, therefore, that a student who is at a standard level of achievement will take a test that is mostly comprised of questions of a standard level; a student who is at an intermediate level of achievement will take a test that is mostly comprised of questions of an intermediate level; and a student who is at an advanced level of achievement will take a test that is mostly comprised of questions of an advanced level.

Do the tests in this book match those in NAPLAN Online?

The practice tests in this book are the same length as in NAPLAN Online. This book provides items across a wide range of difficulty.

Of course there is no way of predicting what actual questions will be asked but practice using these questions will help to familiarise a student with the content of the tests.

Naturally there will be some questions that can be presented on a computer that are harder to present in a book, but the content and skills will be similar.

Like in the NAPLAN Online tests, there are multiple-choice questions in this book but there are some differences. The spelling test is a good example. In the computer version the words are dictated by the computer. We cannot do this in a book but we have prepared a list of words for parents, guardians or teachers to dictate.

Are the questions in this book similar to those in NAPLAN Online?

Parents can have confidence that the questions in this book reflect the online NAPLAN. We believe that we have covered all the types of questions in a convenient book format.

On the whole it is our impression that some of the questions in this book will be much harder than those in NAPLAN. We have deliberately included some more challenging questions.

We have also made a special effort to cover as many different question formats as possible. For instance, spelling questions have been altered to be given orally to the student.

Naturally it is not possible to use the same processes as the online test, such as click and drag, but it is possible to use the same thinking processes.

The Check your skills pages after each test suggest the approximate level of difficulty of questions so you can see what levels of difficulty of questions a student is able to answer.

On the Check your skills pages, questions are divided into standard, intermediate or advanced. This will help you prepare for the standard, intermediate or advanced test that your child will sit. Please refer to page 30 to see an example of a checklist page from the book.

Please refer to the next page to see some examples of question types that are found in NAPLAN Online and how they compare to questions in this book. As you will see, the content tested is exactly the same but the questions are presented differently.

NAPLAN Online question types	Equivalent questions in Reading Tests in this book

Dropdown list
 	
Use the tab to look at Solomon Grundy.
Solomon Grundy is   a poem. ⬇
      a story.
      a book.
	What type of writing is this?
	○ *Solomon Grundy* is a poem.
	○ *Solomon Grundy* is a story.
	○ *Solomon Grundy* is a book.

Identifying/sorting Read ***Healthy Food Builds Healthy Bodies***. Sort these foods to show which are included with cereals: fresh fruit meat, fish and poultry milk, cheese and yoghurt bread, rice and pasta <table><tr><td>Included with cereals</td><td>Not included with cereals</td></tr><tr><td></td><td></td></tr><tr><td></td><td></td></tr><tr><td></td><td></td></tr></table>	To answer this question colour in the circle with the correct answer. What foods are included with cereals? ○ fresh fruit ○ meat, fish and poultry ○ milk, cheese and yoghurt ○ bread, rice and pasta

NAPLAN Online question types	Equivalent questions in Conventions of Language Tests in this book
Drag and drop Drag the correct word to fill in the space. | is		am		be | The big area in the middle of Australia called the outback.	Each sentence has one word or punctuation mark that is incorrect. The mistake in the sentence is underlined. Colour in the circle with the correct answer. The big area in the middle of is am be Australia <u>are</u> called the outback. ○ ○ ○

Click
 	
Which three words should have a capital letter? Click on the words.
 	
The   early   australian   sports   were   a mixture   of   those   from   england   and   ireland.
	Shade three circles to show which words should start with a capital letter.
	
	The early australian sports were a
	  ↑ ↑ ↑ ↑
	  ○ ○ ○ ○
	
	mixture of those from england and ireland.
	    ↑ ↑ ↑
	    ○ ○ ○

NAPLAN Online question types	Equivalent questions in Conventions of Language Tests in this book

Text entry

The poor girl had no _____.

Click on the play button to listen to the missing word.

❚❚ 🔊))) ●————————— 0.08 / 0.09

Type the correct spelling of the word in the box.

Ask your teacher or parent to read the spelling words for you. The words are listed on page 167. Write the spelling words on the lines below.

✏️ **Test 1 spelling words**

26. _____

Spelling words for Conventions of Language Test 1

Word	Example
26. poor	The poor girl had no money.

NAPLAN Online question types	Equivalent questions in Numeracy Tests in this book

Online ruler

How wide is the house in this picture?

Use the online ruler to measure the width of the house.

How wide is it?
- ○ 8 cm
- ○ 4 cm
- ○ 10 cm
- ○ 6 cm

Here is a house. There is a measuring tape underneath. Use this to find the width of the picture.

This tape is marked in metres.

How wide is it?
- ○ 10 metres   ○ 15 metres
- ○ 20 metres   ○ 25 metres

As you can see there are differences between the processes involved in answering the questions in NAPLAN Online and this book but we think they are minimal.

Nevertheless we **strongly advise** that students should practise clicking and dragging until they are **familiar** with using a computer or tablet to answer questions.

What are the advantages of revising for the NAPLAN Online tests in book form?

There are many benefits to a child revising for the online test using books.

- One of the most important benefits is that writing on paper will help your child retain information. It can be a very effective way to memorise. High quality educational research shows that using a keyboard is not as good as note-taking for learning.

- Students will be able to prepare thoroughly for topic revision using books and then practise computer skills easily. They will only succeed with sound knowledge of topics; this requires study and focus. Students will not succeed in tests simply because they know how to answer questions digitally.

- Also, some students find it easier to concentrate when reading a page in a book than when reading on a screen.

- Furthermore it can be more convenient to use a book, especially when a child doesn't have ready access to a digital device.

- You can be confident that **Excel** books will help students acquire the topic knowledge they need, as we have over 30 years experience in helping students prepare for tests. All our writers are experienced educators.

How *Excel Test Zone* can help you practise online

We recommend you go to www.exceltestzone.com.au and register for practice in NAPLAN Online–style tests once you have completed this book. The reasons include:

- for optimal performance in the NAPLAN Online tests we strongly recommend students gain practice at completing online tests as well as completing revision in book form

- students should practise answering questions on a digital device to become confident in this process

- students will be able to practise tailored tests like those in NAPLAN Online as well as other types of tests

- students will also be able to gain valuable practice in onscreen skills such as dragging and dropping answers, using an online ruler to measure figures and using an online protractor to measure angles.

Remember that **Excel Test Zone** has been helping students prepare for NAPLAN since 2009; in fact we had NAPLAN online questions even before NAPLAN tests went online!

We also have updated our website along with our book range to ensure your preparation for NAPLAN Online is 100% up to date.

NAPLAN

What do the tests indicate?

They are designed to be tests of educational achievement; they show what a person has learnt or can do.

They are not IQ tests. Probably boys and girls who do extremely well on these tests will be quite bright. It is possible, however, for some intelligent children to perform poorly because of disadvantage, language, illness or other factors.

Are there time limits?

Yes, there are time limits for each test. These are usually set so that 95% of pupils can complete the tests in the time allowed.

If more than one test is scheduled on a day then there should be a reasonable rest break of at least 20 minutes between tests. In some special cases pupils may be given some extra time and allowed to complete a response.

Who does the NAPLAN Tests?

The NAPLAN Testing Program is held for pupils in Year 3 each year. The tests are designed for all pupils.

Some schools may exempt pupils from the tests. These can include children in special English classes and those who have recently arrived from non–English speaking backgrounds or children with special needs.

Our advice to parents and guardians is that children should only undertake the tests if it is likely to be of benefit to them. It would be a pity if a pupil was not personally or emotionally ready to perform at their best and the results underestimated their ability. The results on this occasion might label them inaccurately and it would be recorded on their pupil record card. Some parents have insisted successfully that their child be exempt from testing.

Who developed these tests?

The tests were developed especially by ACARA. These are large-scale educational tests in which the questions are trialled extensively. Any unsuitable questions will be eliminated in these trials. They should produce results with high validity and reliability.

How can the results be used?

The results of the NAPLAN Tests offer an opportunity to help pupils at an early stage. The findings can be used as early indicators of any problem areas.

It would be a pity to miss this chance to help boys or girls at this stage in their schooling when it is relatively easy to address any issues. The findings can also be used as encouragement for pupils who are performing above the minimum standard.

It is important for parents and teachers to look closely at the student report. This indicates the areas of strength and weakness. The report can be a little complex to read at first but it contains quite a helpful summary of the skills assessed in Reading, Writing, Conventions of Language and Numeracy. Use this as a guide for any revision.

If NAPLAN indicates that there are problems, then repeated testing with other measures of educational achievement is strongly recommended. It is also relevant to compare the results of NAPLAN with general classroom performance.

Remember that all educational test results have limitations. Do not place too much faith in the results of a single assessment.

Does practice help?

There is no benefit in trying to teach to the test because the questions will vary from year to year. Nevertheless a general preparation for the content of NAPLAN Tests should be quite helpful. Some people say that practising such tests is not helpful but we do not agree.

Firstly practice will help to overcome unfamiliarity with test procedures. Secondly it will help pupils deal with specific types of questions. Test practice should help students perform to the best of their ability.

Use the tests in this book to practise test skills and also to diagnose some aspects of learning in Year 3. In saying this parents should make sure their child is interested in undertaking these practice tests. There is no benefit in compelling children to practise.

Sometimes it is easy to forget that they are still young children. We recommend that you sit with them or at least stay nearby while they are completing each test. Give them plenty of praise and encouragement for their efforts.

How are students graded?

One of the big advantages of NAPLAN is that it uses a single scale of achievement. This has 10 levels of achievement that are called bands. It will then be possible for you to see how much progress has been made by each pupil in literacy and numeracy from Year 3 to Year 9. Normally we would expect pupils to increase their level of achievement at each stage. In this book we have tried to grade the questions into levels for you.

Each year covers different bands. In Year 3 there are six achievement bands. Students who are in the lowest band (Band 1) are considered to be below the minimum standard. Students who are at Band 2 in Year 3 are performing at the national minimum standard. Students who are in Bands 3 to 6 are performing above the national minimum standard.

What results are provided to parents?

Parents receive comprehensive test results, as do teachers and schools. These enable interpretation of results at a personal and a group level.

The parent reports will show performance in broad skill bands. Some people will look only at the band reached on these tests but really it is more important to see what the student knows or can do.

The bands covering the middle 60% of the students have been shaded in a lighter colour in the report provided to parents. This is called the average range. But it is quite a large group. There is a huge difference between the pupils who are at the top and bottom of this average range. Averages tend to hide more than they reveal but it will be possible to see whether a pupil is performing above or below the expected range of performance.

Each band will list the child's skills in the area of literacy and numeracy. The results are not straightforward to interpret and some assistance may be required. The bands are not a percentage.

Nevertheless check to see what each pupil knows or can do. See where they need extra help. Look at their strengths in the areas of literacy and numeracy. Then check how the class or school performed and where the pupil is placed within the group as well as in comparison with all other Year 3 pupils. Once again a knowledge of how to interpret test results is required and you should seek assistance. The worst thing to do is to just look at the bands—it is important that these are used for the benefit of each pupil.

Are the tests in Year 3 and Year 5 the same?

The tests increase in difficulty but the general content is much the same. Some questions might be repeated. This is to allow the test developers to standardise the results across Years 3 and 5. The similar questions act like anchors for all the other questions.

When are the tests held?

The tests are planned for May on an agreed date. The actual timetable is listed on the official website at www.nap.edu.au. They may be spread over several days. Ideally the tests should be given in the mornings.

How is NAPLAN related to *My School*?

The My School website reports the NAPLAN results for around 10 000 Australian schools. *My School* is available at www.myschool.edu.au.

Will children be shown what to do?

The testing program is normally very well organised with clear instructions for schools and teachers. Teachers receive special instructions for administering the tests.

Teachers will probably give children practice tests in the weeks before the NAPLAN Tests.

How our book's grading system works

Step 1

In this book you will notice that we have provided Check your skills pages. These pages provide you with information about the content of each question.

Step 2

Once you have completed the checklists you will be able to see the content that was easy for the student or the questions that were difficult.

How to proceed

We recommend that you sit with each student using this book or remain nearby to answer any questions or to provide encouragement. Do not leave them alone.

1. Start with the sample questions.

Work with each child. Explain to them how to answer a multiple-choice question. They may have never seen one previously. Tell them that they have to choose the correct answer. Explain that only one of the options is correct.

Show them how and where to write an answer if it is an open-ended question. Be patient if they do not understand at first.

2. Proceed to the practice tests.

Once you have covered the sample questions it is time to proceed to the practice tests. Do not attempt more than one practice test in one sitting. Remember that these are still young children and that they tire easily.

3. Stop when you reach the maximum level of performance.

When you realise that a child has reached their maximum level of performance in a practice test it is time to stop. Do not force children to try to go beyond their level. They may find it difficult because they might not have covered this content yet in Year 3. It may be beyond their natural ability at present and setting it aside for even a few months will allow them time to mature in their thinking and development. This is because there will be substantial increases in educational development, comprehension and understanding in Year 3. Some tasks that may be difficult at the outset will become easier later in the year.

• • • • • • • •

Please note that it is not possible to accurately predict the content of the NAPLAN Tests. NAPLAN focuses on the 'essential elements that should be taught at the appropriate year levels'.

Thank you for your patience in working through this introduction. We hope you find this guide helpful. It is designed to be easy to use and to help pupils prepare. We wish every pupil well in the NAPLAN Tests and in their future studies.

**Associate Professor James A Athanasou, LittB, MA, PhD, DipEd, MAPS
Angella Deftereos, BA, MTeach**

INSTRUCTIONS FOR PARENTS AND TEACHERS USING THIS BOOK

How is this book organised?

It is divided into sample questions and practice tests. We start with samples of the numeracy and literacy (reading and conventions of language) questions. Work through these examples so that every student knows what needs to be done. At the very least please ensure that your child is familiar with the sample questions.

This is followed by four practice tests for numeracy, four practice tests for reading and four practice tests for conventions of language. There is also a sample writing task and four practice tests for writing. At the very least try to revise the samples if you do not have enough time to do the practice tests.

Numeracy Tests

The Numeracy Tests in this book have 36 questions. They should take 45 minutes. Some children will finish quickly while others will need all the time available.

Try not to explain terms during the testing. This can be done after the test session. If a question is still too hard, it is better to leave it at this stage. Some students may not be ready for the task.

Literacy Tests

Literacy is divided into three tests: Reading, Conventions of Language and Writing.

The Writing Test offers help with aspects of writing using prompts and stimulus materials.

Allow up to 45 minutes for Reading Tests, 45 minutes for Conventions of Language Tests and 40 minutes for Writing Tests, with a break in between.

- In the Reading Test students will read stories, letters and non-fiction writing. There will be supporting pictures and charts. Students will be asked to find information, make conclusions, find the meaning and look at different ideas.

- The Conventions of Language Test is divided into two parts: grammar and punctuation, and spelling. Students must be able to use verbs and punctuation, such as speech marks and commas, correctly. Also they will be asked to spell words.

- In the Writing Test students will write a specific type of text. They will be judged on the structure of their writing, as well as their grammar, punctuation and spelling.

Test materials

All test materials are contained in this book. There are answers for scoring the responses.

Equipment

Students will not need white-out, pens or calculators. It is best to use a pencil. Children should be provided with a pencil, an eraser and a blank sheet of paper for working out.

Time limits

Try to keep roughly to the time limits for the tests. You may give some students extra time if they are tired. Even a short break every 20 minutes is appropriate.

Instructions to students

Explain patiently what needs to be done. Students should only attempt these tests if they wish to and do no more than one test in a session.

Recording answers

Show students the way to mark the answers. They have to colour in circles, shapes or numbers, or write the answers in the boxes or on the lines provided.

SAMPLE QUESTIONS—NUMERACY

Here are some sample Numeracy questions. Make sure you read each question carefully so that you know exactly:
- what information is given to you in the question
- what the question is asking you to find.

Then make sure you read each answer option carefully in order to choose the correct answer. There is no time limit for the sample questions.

If you aren't sure what to do, ask your teacher or your parents to help you. Don't be afraid to ask if it isn't clear to you. There is no time limit for the sample questions.

To answer these questions, write the answer in the box or colour in the circle with the correct answer. Colour in only one circle for each answer.

1. Which of these groups shows the number 11?

○   ○   ○   ○

Did you colour in one of the circles?

2. Which number is the largest?

54   45   64   61

○   ○   ○   ○

3. Which is the tallest house?

○   ○   ○   ○

4. Which object is a cube?

○   ○   ○   ○

5. I folded this pattern in half.

Fold here

Which shape could I see?

○   ○   ○   ○

6. How much do these coins add up to?

85c $1.55 $1.75 $1.85

○   ○   ○   ○

7. There are 15 candles. Each child is given three candles.

How many children will get candles?

6   3   8   5

○   ○   ○   ○

8. This table shows the number of cars in each family.

Family	Number of cars
Rooney	3
Collier	2
Flowers	3
Hager	1
Pennycook	2

How many cars do the Rooney family and the Flowers family have altogether?

[   ] cars

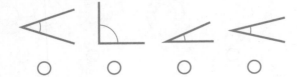
Write your answer in the box.

9. Which is the largest angle?

○   ○   ○   ○

10. Here is a map of Tasmania. It shows five locations. The map is divided into sections marked 1, 2, 3, 4 along the side and A, B, C, D along the bottom.

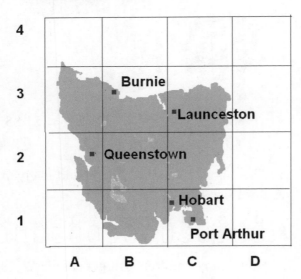

Which city is in B3?

○ Burnie

○ Queenstown

○ Launceston

○ Hobart

11. Where is Port Arthur on the grid?

C1   A2   B3   C3

○   ○   ○   ○

12. A packet of chips costs $2. A boy buys 5 packets of chips.

Fill in the number sentence below. Show how much he spent.

$ [   ] × 5 = $ [   ]

Write your answers in the boxes.

13. Here are some objects. There is a top row and a bottom row.

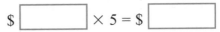

Which object is in the top row second from the left?

envelope   bell   clock   pencil

○   ○   ○   ○

14. What time does this clock show?

12:00   3:00   3:15   9:00

○   ○   ○   ○

15. There is a picture that covers some squares. How many pictures like this one are needed to cover all the area? (Hint: use the size of the first picture to help you. Remember to include the picture that is shown in the final total.)

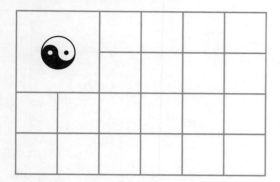

How many pictures are needed?

☐ pictures

Write your answer in the box.

16. Name the main shapes that make up this figure.

○ diamonds
○ squares
○ triangles
○ rectangles

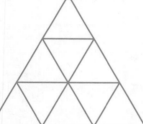

You are about halfway through the sample questions—well done!

---

17. Look at the example below. The number 0 looks the same when it is flipped or turned over.

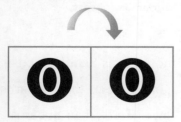

Now look at this example. The number 3 is not the same when it is flipped or turned over.

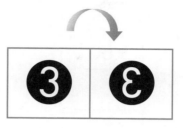

Which of these numbers will look the same if it is flipped or turned over?

○   ○   ○   ○

18. Look at these 2 trucks. The first one carries 24 computers. The second truck carries 36 computers.

How many more computers are there in the second truck compared to the first?

60   12   8   16
○   ○   ○   ○

19. Break each shape into quarters. How many parts would you have in total?

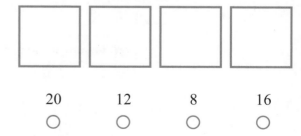

20   12   8   16
○   ○   ○   ○

20. There is a pattern in these numbers. Write in the number that is missing.

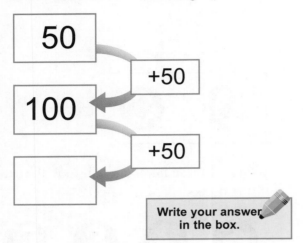

Write your answer in the box.

21. What shapes should come next in this pattern?

◆◆✠✠ℭℭℭℭ◆◆✠✠ℭℭℭℭ◆◆

ℭℭℭ   ✠✠✠   ℭℭℭℭ   ✠✠✠✠
 ○   ○   ○   ○

22. Use the calendar below to answer the next question.

JANUARY

Sun	Mon	Tue	Wed	Thur	Fri	Sat
				1	2	3
4	5	6	7	8	9	10
11	12	13	14	15	16	17
18	19	20	21	22	23	24
25	26	27	28	29	30	31

How many days are there from 4 to 19 January?

Write your answer in the box.

23. Here is a shape made out of some blocks.

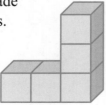

Which one of the 4 shapes below is the same as the one shown? Is it A, B, C or D?

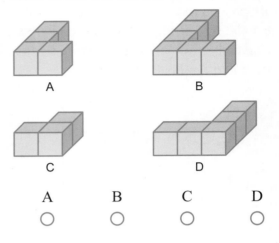

A	B	C	D
○	○	○	○

24. This toy car costs $2.50.

How much will three toy cars cost?

Write your answer in the box.

25. This chart shows the number of cars in our street.

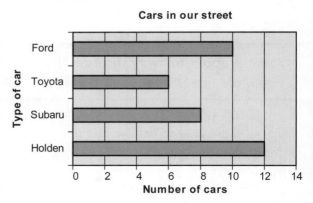

Which answer is correct?

○ There are more Fords than Holdens.

○ There are more Toyotas than Subarus.

○ There are fewer Fords than Subarus.

○ There are fewer Toyotas than Subarus.

26. Here is a chart of how people voted in an election.

Obama	XXXXXXXXXX
Bush	XXX
McCain	XXXXXXX
Clinton	XXXXXX

Each X stands for 10 people.

How many people voted for Obama?

[   ] people

Write your answer in the box.

27. Here is a shape. Some parts are coloured and some are blank.

How many parts are coloured?

- ○ 4 out of 7 parts
- ○ 4 out of 4 parts
- ○ 3 out of 7 parts
- ○ 3 out of 3 parts

28. There are 4 parking lots in an airport for planes. The parking lots are called A, B, C and D.

One of them is only one-quarter full.

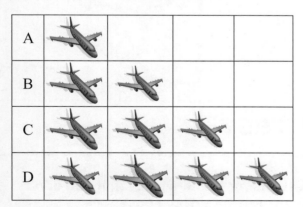

Which parking lot is one-quarter full?

A	B	C	D
○	○	○	○

29. Here is a shape made from different pieces. How many of the pieces are triangular prisms?

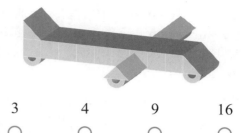

3	4	9	16
○	○	○	○

30. There are 22 dollars to be divided between John and Jane. John has to receive 4 dollars more than Jane.

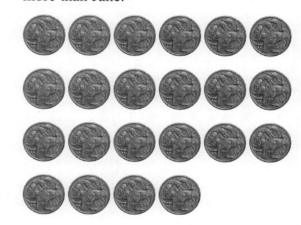

How much will each person get?

Jane: [   ] dollars

John: [   ] dollars

Write your answers in the boxes.

31. Here are four groups of three people.

The total number of people is equal to:

4 + 3	4 − 3	4 × 3	4 ÷ 3
○	○	○	○

32. Imagine a calculator that gives all answers to end in either 0 or 5.

If the sum was 6 + 5 then it would give a result of 10 because 10 is closest to 11. If the sum was 6 + 7 it would give a result of 15 because the true answer of 13 is closest to 15.

What answer would it give for 27 + 36?

55	60	65	70
○	○	○	○

33. Draw a chart which shows the pattern in these numbers. What will the next pattern look like?

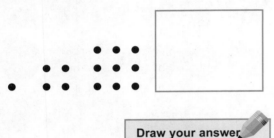

Draw your answer in the box.

34. There is a pattern in these numbers. Write the number that is missing.

5   12   19   [   ]   33

Write your answer in the box.

35. I left home at 8 am. I take exactly an hour to travel to school.

My digital watch is 10 minutes fast. What time will it show?

9:10	8:50	9:00	10:10
○	○	○	○

END OF TEST

Well done! You have completed the sample questions for Numeracy. Even if you don't practise any others, at least you will have done a fair sample of the questions.

How did you go with these sample questions? Check to see where you did well and where you had problems. Try to revise the questions that were hard for you.

There are four more Numeracy Tests to practise, each containing 36 questions. They include many of the same types of questions, plus a few other types.

1. The **second group** is the number 11. This should have been easy for you.

2. The largest number is **64**. If you want to change your answer just erase it and colour in the circle you want.

3. The **third house** is the tallest. Did you pick this easily?

4. The cube is the **first** object.

5. The **first answer** is correct. We have tried to show this below (it is not drawn to scale). When you put both halves together then you get a circle.

6. **$1.85**. The coins are
$5c + 10c + 20c + 50c + \$1 = \$1.85$.

7. **5**. There are 15 candles and each child is given three candles. So there must be five children $(3 + 3 + 3 + 3 + 3 = 15$ or $15 \div 3 = 5)$.

8. **6**. The Rooney family have three cars and the Flowers family have three cars and this makes **six** cars altogether. Did you write your answer in the space provided?

9. The **second answer** is correct. It is the largest angle. The space between the lines is widest. Don't let the length of the lines confuse you. It is the size of the opening that is important.

10. **Burnie** is in B3. Remember to count across the bottom first then count upwards.

11. Port Arthur is in the square or cell called **C1**.

12. **$2 \times 5 = \$10$**. The chips cost $2. The boy buys five packets, so the sum is $\$2 \times 5 = \$10$. Did you write your answer in the space provided?

13. The **pencil** is in the top row and second from the left.

14. **3:00**. The time is three o'clock.

15. **6**. There are 24 squares and each picture covers four squares.

16. They are all **triangles**.

17. **❽**. The number **❽** looks the same when it is turned over horizontally. This is what we mean by *flipped over*.

18. **12**. The second truck has 36 computers and this is 12 more than the first truck. It is:
$36 - 24 = 12$.

19. **16**. Each square would be divided into four and then there would be $4 \times 4 = 16$ pieces.

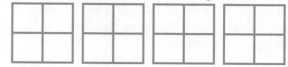

20. **150**. The numbers increase by 50. We start with 50 then add 50 to make 100. Then we add 50 to 100 to make 150. Did you write your answer in the rectangle?

21. **✠✠✠**. The pattern is quite simple: there are two ◆◆ then three ✠✠✠ and then four ⚲⚲⚲⚲. After the ◆ symbol, then, comes the ✠ symbol.

22. **15 days**. There are 15 days from the 4th to the 19th January $(19 - 4 = 15)$.

23. **D**. This is L-shaped with five blocks. The others are quite different.

24. **$7.50**. Each car costs $2.50 so the sum is $\$2.50 \times 3 = \$7.50$.

25. **There are fewer Toyotas than Subarus**. There were six Toyotas and eight Subarus.

26. **100**. There are ten Xs. Each X stands for 10 people so the sum is $10 \times 10 = 100$.

27. **4 out of 7 parts**. You need to count the parts and then decide how many are coloured.

28. **A**. This has only one plane in the four spaces so it is one-quarter full.

29. **4**. There are four triangular prisms. There is one at the nose of the aeroplane, one for each wing and one for the tail of the aeroplane.

30. **Jane 9 dollars and John 13 dollars**. This is because $9 + 13 = 22$ and the difference between them had to be four dollars.

31. **4×3**. The total number of people is equal to 4×3 because there are four groups of three people.

32. **65**. The true answer to the sum $27 + 36$ is 63 and the closest number ending in a 0 or a 5 is 65.

33. **16 dots**. These are squares. We started with 1×1, then 2×2, then 3×3 and then 4×4 or 16 dots. Get someone to explain this to you if our explanation is not clear.

34. **26**. The pattern is 5, 12, 19, 26 then 33. The numbers increase by 7.

35. **9:10**. I leave home at 8 am and it takes an hour to travel so I get there at 9 am. My watch is 10 minutes fast so it will show 9:10.

Here are some sample Reading questions. You will need to look at or read a text. Make sure you read each question carefully so that you know exactly what the question is asking. Then find the relevant section in the text. Finally make sure you read each answer option carefully in order to choose the correct answer. There is no time limit for the sample questions.

To answer these questions, write the answer in the box or colour in the circle with the correct answer. Colour in only one circle for each answer.

If you aren't sure what to do, ask your teacher or your parents to help you. Don't be afraid to ask if it isn't clear to you.

---

1. Look at the diagram below and answer question 1. Which part does not match the label? Colour in only one answer.

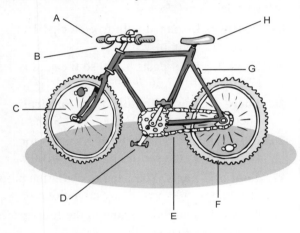

- ○ A   handle bars
- ○ B   bell
- ○ C   spokes
- ○ D   pedal
- ○ E   chain
- ○ F   tyre
- ○ G   reflector
- ○ H   seat

Did you colour in one of the circles?

Look at the book cover and answer questions 2 to 4.

From *Art Today*, CD1/0031/BWC078A.JPG

2. Who wrote this book?
- ○ Jane L Stewart
- ○ The Camp Fire Girls
- ○ Girl Guides

3. What is this text about?
- ○ It is a book about women campers.
- ○ It is a book about boy scouts and girl guides.
- ○ It is a book about girl campers.

4. What would you read about in this book?
- ○ You would read about cooking at a camp.
- ○ You would read about bushwalking.
- ○ You would read about bushfires.

Look at the cartoon and answer questions 5 to 7.

From *Art Today*, CD3/0163/AGH296B/C/D/G/.JPG

5. What is happening in this cartoon?

  ○ The man is helping the painter.

  ○ The man is being cheeky and annoying the painter.

  ○ The painter is angry because the man is whistling.

6. What does the sign FRESH PAINT mean?

  ○ It means that the tin of paint is new.

  ○ It means that the paint is still wet.

  ○ It means that he is about to paint.

7. What does the painter do in this cartoon?

  ○ The painter puts up the sign; checks to see that the paint is not touched; sees the man touching the wet paint; and gets angry with the man.

  ○ The painter puts up the sign; speaks to the man; sees the man touching the wet paint; and gets angry with the man.

  ○ The painter puts up the sign; checks to see that the paint is not touched; listens to the man whistling; and gets angry with the man.

Did you colour in one of the circles?

Read *Trees* and answer questions 8 to 14.

Trees

A tree is a plant with a tall, woody trunk. Like all plants, trees need air, water and sunlight to live and grow.

A tree has a long, woody trunk covered in bark. The trunk supports the branches, putting them high above the ground. Bark is dead and protects the living trunk inside. The trunk grows thicker and taller each year.

Trees have many branches. Tree branches spread out in all directions towards sunlight. More and more branches grow each year.

Leaves grow on the branches. The leaves cover the tree in a canopy of green. Leaves use the sun's energy to make food for the whole tree.

The tree has roots under the ground. Roots absorb water and nutrients from the soil. Trees need water to live and grow. The roots also hold the tree firm when the wind blows.

From *Go Facts: Trees*, Blake Publishing, 2000

8. What would be another good title for this text?
   - ○ How a Tree Grows
   - ○ What is a Tree?
   - ○ The Story of Trees
   - ○ Kinds of Trees

9. Where would you see a passage like this?
   - ○ on the Internet
   - ○ in a newspaper
   - ○ in a book
   - ○ on a poster

10. Which sentence is wrong?
    - ○ Trees need air, water and sunlight to live and grow.
    - ○ Bark is dead.
    - ○ The trunk uses the sun's energy to make food for the whole tree.
    - ○ The tree has roots under the ground.

11. Which word is similar in meaning to *canopy*?
    - ○ shelter
    - ○ revealing
    - ○ circle
    - ○ partition

12. The word *absorb* means
    - ○ to choose.
    - ○ to need.
    - ○ to give away.
    - ○ to soak up.

13. What is the purpose of the leaves on a tree?
    - ○ The leaves protect the trunk.
    - ○ The leaves hold the tree firm when the wind blows.
    - ○ The leaves help get water and nutrients from the soil.
    - ○ The leaves help make food for the tree.

14. Find a rhyming word from the passage for these words. Write your answers on the lines below.

    bunk   _____

    dark   _____

    deer   _____

    found   _____

    boil   _____

15. Below are the stages of the life cycle of a tree, but they are not in the correct order. Put them in the correct order. Write the numbers 1 to 4 in the boxes.

    > Write your answers in the boxes.

    ☐ When the tree is mature it flowers. New seeds grow from the flowers.

    ☐ Small roots grow down into the ground reaching for water. A green shoot grows up into the sunlight. The young tree must begin to make its own food.

    ☐ The life of a new tree starts when a seed drops from a branch. It may drop to the ground or be carried away by an animal, by wind, or by water. A seed needs water and warmth to begin to grow.

    ☐ Young trees are called saplings. Saplings grow straight and tall towards sunlight.

    You are about halfway through the sample questions—well done!

Read *The Ants and the Grasshopper* and answer questions 16 to 21.

The Ants and the Grasshopper

One bright day in late autumn a family of Ants were bustling about in the warm sunshine, drying out the grain they had stored up during the summer, when a starving Grasshopper, his fiddle under his arm, came up and humbly begged for a bite to eat.

"What!" cried the Ants in surprise, "Haven't you stored anything away for the winter? What in the world were you doing all last summer?"

"I didn't have time to store up any food," whined the Grasshopper. "I was so busy making music that before I knew it the summer was gone."

The Ants shrugged their shoulders in disgust.

"Making music, were you?" they cried. "Very well; now dance!" And they turned their backs on the Grasshopper and went on with their work.

From The Gutenberg Project e-book of *The Aesop for Children With Pictures* by Milo Winter, Rand McNally, 1919

16. What is the title of this passage?

○ One bright day in Autumn

○ The Aesop for Children

○ The Ants and the Grasshopper

17. In which season did the story occur?

○ Spring

○ Summer

○ Autumn

○ Winter

18. Why was the grasshopper so hungry? Write your answer on the lines.

_____

_____

_____

_____

_____

19. What is the purpose of this story?

○ The purpose of this story is to inform.

○ The purpose of this story is to advertise.

○ The purpose of this story is to entertain.

○ The purpose of this story is to teach.

20. What does the word *whined* mean?

○ complained

○ groaned

○ drank

○ suggested

21. What is the hidden meaning of this story?

○ The hidden meaning of this story is that grasshoppers are lazy.

○ The hidden meaning of this story is that ants are hard working.

○ The hidden meaning of this story is that we should save while we have the chance.

○ The hidden meaning of this story is that we should work hard and not play music.

Read *Giant Pandas* and answer questions 22 to 25.

Giant Pandas

Panda Facts

- Giant pandas are part of the bear family.
- Only about 1500 giant pandas remain in the wild.
- Giant pandas have a sixth claw, like a thumb, used mainly to grasp bamboo.

Conservation Concerns

Endangered due to humans taking over much of their environment.

Range

Central and Western China.

Habitat

Giant pandas live in bamboo forests. They used to be found in China, Myanmar and Vietnam, but now are mainly found in Southwest China.

Size

Height: 1.2 to 1.5 m

Weight: 80 to 160 kg

Appearance

The giant panda looks like other bears except it has black patches over its eyes, ears, legs and shoulders.

Feeding Habits

Giant pandas are herbivores. They mainly eat bamboo. They spend about 10 to 16 hours eating each day. Giant pandas eat about 12 kg of bamboo a day.

Offspring

Giant pandas mate between March and May. Females give birth to one or two cubs about 3–6 months later.

Life Span

About 20 to 30 years.

22. Why are the giant pandas losing their habitats?

- ○ They eat about 12 kg of bamboo a day.
- ○ The zoos are closing down.
- ○ They have been burnt down.
- ○ Humans are taking over their environment.

23. Colour in the statements that are true. (You can colour in more than one.)

- ○ Giant pandas can weigh up to 160 kg.
- ○ Giant pandas have six thumbs.
- ○ There are about 1500 pandas left in the wild.
- ○ Giant pandas can be found in China, Myanmar and Vietnam.
- ○ Giant pandas are brown and white.
- ○ Giant pandas are an endangered species.
- ○ Giant pandas live to be about 20 to 30 years old.
- ○ Giant pandas are carnivores (meat-eaters).

24. What is the author's purpose in this text?

- ○ The author's purpose is to entertain.
- ○ The author's purpose is to persuade.
- ○ The author's purpose is to inform.
- ○ The author's purpose is to advertise.

25. How many hours a day does a panda spend eating?

- ○ 10 to 16 hours
- ○ 12 to 16 hours
- ○ 3 to 6 hours
- ○ 20 to 30 hours

A table of contents can be found at the beginning of a book. It may list the title of the book, as well as the name of each chapter and on which page it begins. Read the table of contents from the book *Wild Animals* and answer questions 26 to 28.

Wild Animals

Table of contents

26. How many chapters are there in this book?

9   10   11   12
○   ○   ○   ○

27. What is the title of the fourth chapter?

○ Are there killer cats?

○ How loud is a lion's roar?

○ Do hyenas laugh?

○ Can any animal outrun a cheetah?

28. On which page can you find information on tigers?

7   25   19   12
○   ○   ○   ○

Read the text and answer questions 29 to 32.

"This bridge links the north and south parts of the city. It opened on 19 March 1932 and is the largest bridge in Australia. There are six million rivets and 52 800 tonnes of steel. 150 000 vehicles cross it every day," she said.

"It takes ten years and 30 000 litres to paint the whole bridge. So as soon as the painters finish they have to start all over again."

On and on went the tour lady as they climbed. Then she stopped and finally drew a breath, "Here we are ladies and gentlemen! The best view in town."

Ella and Dom looked up. They were at the very top of the Sydney Harbour Bridge! The view was a knockout. Ella forgot all about her fear of heights.

From *SWAT: Sent to Sydney* by Lisa Thompson, Blake Education, 2000

29. What would be a good title for this passage?

○ Our Holiday

○ The Sydney Harbour Bridge

○ The Best View in Town

○ Ella and Dom's Adventure

30. How many vehicles cross the Bridge every day?

○ 150 000

○ 30 000

○ 52 800

○ six million

31. *Ella and Dom looked up.* This is

○ a statement.

○ a question.

○ an explanation.

○ a command.

32. Find a rhyming word from the text for these words. Write your answers on the lines provided.

fridge _____

death _____

new _____

Read *Kalvin Costi* and answer question 33.

Kalvin Costi

Born 18.1.55, he sang in a band and had a number one hit in Japan in 1970. He starred in the movies *California Beach* and *The Fox*. He directed and acted in the award-winning film *Dances with Penguins*. He then followed with *ZFX*, *Underwaterworld* and *Your Place*.

33. Colour in the statements which are true. (Hint: more than one statement is correct.)

○ Kalvin Costi is a singer.

○ Kalvin Costi is an actor and director.

○ Kalvin Costi was born in Japan.

○ Kalvin Costi likes dancing with penguins.

○ Kalvin Costi won an award for his movie *ZFX*.

○ Kalvin Costi appeared in six movies.

END OF TEST

Well done! You have completed the sample questions for Reading. Even if you don't practise any other Reading Tests, at least you will have done a fair sample of the questions.

How did you go with these sample questions? Check to see where you did well and where you had problems. Try to revise the questions that were hard for you.

There are four more Reading Tests to practise, each containing just under 40 questions. They include many of the same types of questions, plus a few other types.

The spelling, grammar and punctuation questions are in the Conventions of Language sample test. You can do this test now or you can leave it until later. Now take a break before you start any more tests.

1. **B—bell**. These are the brakes of the bike, not the bell. Did you colour in the circle for B? Do you know what to do if you change your mind? Just erase the wrong answer and then change your answer. Do not leave two answers coloured in—remember to erase one of them.

2. **Jane L Stewart**

3. **It is a book about girl campers.** Remember: in this test you should guess if you are not sure.

4. **You would read about cooking at a camp.**

5. **The man is being cheeky and annoying the painter.**

6. **It means that the paint is still wet.**

7. **The painter puts up the sign; checks to see that the paint is not touched; sees the man touching the wet paint; and gets angry with the man.**

8. **What is a Tree?** This is the actual title of the passage. Did you remember to colour in only one of the circles?

9. You would normally see a passage like this **in a book**.

10. **The trunk uses the sun's energy to make food for the whole tree.** The leaves, and not the trunk, use the sun's energy to make food for the tree.

11. *Canopy* means **shelter**. You may not have seen the word before.

12. The word *absorb* means **to soak up**.

13. **The leaves help make food for the tree.**

14. **Trunk** rhymes with bunk.
    Bark rhymes with dark.
    Year rhymes with deer.
    Ground rhymes with found.
    Soil rhymes with boil.

15. **1.** The life of a new tree starts when a seed drops from a branch. It may drop to the ground or be carried away by an animal, by wind, or by water. A seed needs water and warmth to begin to grow.

    2. Small roots grow down into the ground reaching for water. A green shoot grows up into the sunlight. The young tree must begin to make its own food.

    3. Young trees are called saplings. Saplings grow straight and tall towards sunlight.

    4. When the tree is mature it flowers. New seeds grow from the flowers.

This may have been a hard question for you. Remember to ask for help if you are not sure of the answers.

16. The title of this passage is **The Ants and the Grasshopper**. This should have been easy for you.

17. **Autumn.**

18. He was so hungry because he had not **stored anything away.**

19. **The purpose of this story is to teach.**

20. **complained.** *To whine* means 'to complain or moan about something'. This may have been a little tricky for you. Remember to ask someone if you are not sure. It is not a problem if you have to use a dictionary to find the meaning. The aim of these questions is to help you learn, not to practise answers.

21. **The hidden meaning of this story is that we should save while we have the chance.**

22. Giant pandas are losing their habitats because **humans are taking over their environment**.

23. **Giant pandas can weigh up to 160 kg. There are about 1500 pandas left in the wild. Giant pandas are an endangered species. Giant pandas live to be about 20 to 30 years old.**

24. **The author's purpose is to inform**.

25. Giant pandas eat for **10 to 16 hours** a day.

26. There are **10** chapters in this book.

27. The title of the fourth chapter is **'Can any animal outrun a cheetah?'**

28. Information on tigers can be found on page **25** in the chapter titled 'How big is a tiger's paw?'

29. A good title for this passage would be **The Sydney Harbour Bridge**.

30. **150 000**

31. This is **a statement**. This may have been difficult for you. If you are not certain which answer to choose, eliminate those answers that you are sure are wrong and then make a guess from those that are left over.

32. **Bridge** rhymes with fridge.
    Breath rhymes with death.
    View rhymes with new.

33. **Kalvin Costi is a singer.**
    Kalvin Costi is an actor and director.
    Kalvin Costi appeared in six movies.

Instructions for parents and teachers

This section tests whether students can spell words and find spelling, grammar and punctuation errors in a text.

The first series of questions are grammar and punctuation questions just as in NAPLAN Online. Then we have provided spelling words that are to be read out to the student. The words are read by a teacher or parent. The student writes their answer on the lines we have provided below. This is similar to NAPLAN Online.

Read the sentences. They have some gaps. Colour in the circle with the correct answer. Colour in only one circle for each answer.

1. Tuesday _____ another of our special days.

   has ○   is ○

2. Dieu was class monitor last _____ .

   weak ○   week ○

3. _____ teaches Grade 4.

   Mrs bramble ○   Mrs Bramble ○   mrs bramble ○

4. Pat _____ how they laughed at her joke.

   remember ○   remembered ○

5. You can see the _____ in the back garden.

   goanna ○   Goanna ○

6. _____ dog is black, brown and white.

   Marios ○   Mario's ○   Marios' ○

7. The quick brown fox jumped _____ the lazy dog.

   in ○   under ○   over ○

8. _____ played tennis in the street.

   david ○   David ○   Davids ○

Colour in the circle with the correct answer.

9 Where should the speech marks (") go?

"Hello, said Mr Smith .

10. Where do the capital letters go? Colour in more than one bubble.

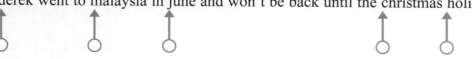

derek went to malaysia in june and won't be back until the christmas holidays.

11. Where does the apostrophe (') go?

The elephant swayed its trunk at my brothers friends.

12. Shade **three** circles to show where the apostrophes (') should go.

Its impossible for Jims cousins to come to his grandmothers house.

Sample spelling questions

To the teacher or parent

First read and say the word slowly and clearly. Then read the sentence with the word in it. Then repeat the word again.

If the student is not sure, ask them to guess. It is okay to skip a word if it is not known.

Sample spelling words

Word	Example
13. car	My car is red.
14. cow	A cow gives milk.
15. book	At school I read a book.
16. fish	The fish swims in the sea.
17. bus	There are many people on the bus.
18. told	He told me a story.
19. mango	A mango is a fruit.
20. donkey	A donkey is a hardworking animal.
21. blanket	I cover myself with a blanket.
22. night	It is dark at night.
23. baby	We have a new baby in our house.
24. skirt	Jane wore a skirt to the party.

Write your answer on the line.

13. _____   19. _____

14. _____   20. _____

15. _____   21. _____

16. _____   22. _____

17. _____   23. _____

18. _____   24. _____

SAMPLE QUESTIONS—CONVENTIONS OF LANGUAGE

The spelling mistakes in these sentences have been underlined. Write the correct spelling of the word in the box.

25. Many <u>anemals</u> live in trees.

26. Trees provide food and <u>shelta</u>.

27. Most monkeys <u>fined</u> food in trees.

28. Their <u>homs</u> are above the ground.

29. Monkeys are used to <u>liffe</u> in the trees.

30. Their <u>tales</u> help them to climb.

There is one spelling mistake in each sentence. Write the correct spelling of the word in the box.

31. The Gold Coast had 35 beeches and tropical rainforests.

32. There are national parks, mounten villages and spectacular views.

33. You can visit kraft shops.

34. There are many parks for barbecues and pikniks.

Read the text *A Scare at the Beach*. Each line has one word that is incorrect.
Write the correct spelling of the word in the box.

A Scare at the Beach

35. An ionman champion was pushed off his
    surfboard by a shark.

36. Bystanders thort the shark was around
    three metres long.

37. They saw two otha large sharks.

38. A helicopter chaised away the other sharks.

END OF TEST

Well done! You have completed the sample questions for Conventions of Language.
Even if you don't practise any more Conventions of Language Tests, at least you will
have done a fair sample of the questions.

How did you go with these sample questions? Check to see where you did well and where
you had problems. Try to revise the questions that were hard for you.

There are four more Conventions of Language Tests to practise. These are longer and
contain around 50 questions. They include many of the same types of questions, plus a
few other types.

1. **is**
2. **week**
3. **Mrs Bramble**
4. **remembered**
5. **goanna.** If you aren't sure about an answer, just guess. If you have time, you can come back to these questions at the end.
6. **Mario's**
7. **over.** Ask your teacher or parents why this is an unusual sentence. Hint: see if it uses every letter in the alphabet.
8. **David.** Please note that there are no tricks intended in any of these questions. In the NAPLAN Tests, the questions are specially selected and designed to test your knowledge.
9. **"Hello", said Mr Smith.** We have underlined the changes for you to make it easier to see. This has also been done in the next three questions.
10. **Derek went to Malaysia in June and won't be back until the Christmas holidays.**
11. **The elephant swayed its trunk at my brother's friends.** *Brother's* needs an apostrophe because it shows possession or ownership: the friends belong to the brother. We hope that you didn't put an apostrophe for *its*. The difference between *its* and *it's* is still not clear for many adults, so you have done well if you recognised this.
12. **It's impossible for Jim's cousins to come to his grandmother's house.** *It's* is an abbreviation of the words *it is*; *Jim's* and *grandmother's* show possession or ownership. Watch out for apostrophes—even adults make mistakes with them.
13. **car**
14. **cow**
15. **book**
16. **fish**
17. **bus**
18. **told**
19. **mango**
20. **donkey**
21. **blanket**
22. **night**
23. **baby**
24. **skirt**
25. **animals**
26. **shelter**
27. **find**
28. **homes**
29. **life**
30. **tails**
31. **beaches**
32. **mountain**
33. **craft**
34. **picnics**
35. **ironman.** Don't spend too much time on any one question. Allow around one minute for each question.
36. **thought**
37. **other**
38. **chased**

This is the first Numeracy Test. There are 36 questions.

If you aren't sure what to do, ask your teacher or your parents to help you. Don't be afraid to ask if it isn't clear to you.

Allow around 45 minutes for this test.

Write the answer in the box or colour in the circle with the correct answer. Colour in only one circle for each answer.

1. Look at the ✳ shapes. Count how many there are. Then write how many TENS and ONES there are.

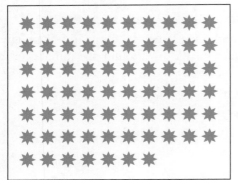

TENS	
ONES	

Write your answers in the boxes.

2. Which number is the largest?

369   693   396   963
○   ○   ○   ○

3. Which is the longest piece of wood?

○

○

○

○

4. Which object is a cylinder?

○   ○   ○   ○

5. I cut this white shape out of the orange paper. Then I folded the paper in half.

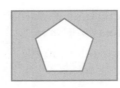 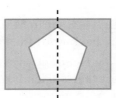

Which shape should I see?

○   ○   ○   ○

Did you colour in one of the circles?

6. How much do these coins make altogether?

$3.70	83c	$8.30	$3.80
○	○	○	○

7. Count the crayons. Each child is given four crayons.

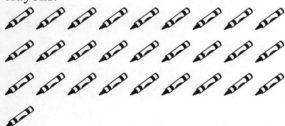

How many children will get crayons?

5	6	7	8
○	○	○	○

8. This table shows the number of points for each country in football.

Team	Number of points
Austria	8
France	10
Italy	6
Germany	7
Spain	4

Which team is in third place?

Austria	Spain	Germany	Italy
○	○	○	○

9. Here are four angles. The angle is shown with a dot. Which is the largest angle?

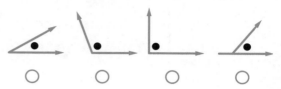

○	○	○	○

10. Here is a chart. It shows four pictures at different positions in the chart. The map is divided into sections marked 1, 2, 3, 4 along the side and A, B, C, D along the bottom.

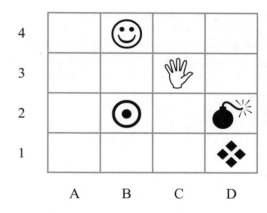

Which picture is in B2?

○	○	○	○

11. Each car has four wheels.

Fill in the number sentence below to show how many wheels there are.

[　　] × 4 = [　　] wheels

> **Write your answers in the boxes.**

12. Here is some information to answer a question.

> **The match was last Monday.**
>
> **Today is Thursday 18 July.**

When was the match?

○ The match is on 22 July.

○ The match is on 15 July.

○ The match is on 16 July.

○ The match is on 14 July.

> **It would be a good idea to check your answers to questions 1 to 12 before moving on to the other questions.**

13. Here is a digital clock.

Which clock shows this time?

○   ○   ○   ○

14. There is a picture that covers some squares. How many pictures like this one are needed to cover all the area? (Hint: use the size of the first picture to help you. Remember to include the picture that is shown in the final total.)

How many pictures are needed?

[   ] pictures

> Write your answer in the box.

15. Look at this calendar.

May						
M	**T**	**W**	**T**	**F**	**S**	**S**
1	2	3	4	5	6	7
8	9	10	11	12	13	14
15	16	17	18	19	20	21
22	23	24	25	26	27	28
29	30	31				

How many weeks are there from 4 May to 25 May?

1 week   2 weeks   3 weeks   4 weeks

○   ○   ○   ○

16. Which of these shapes would look the same if it was flipped horizontally (sideways)?

○   ○   ○   ○

17. Look at these two ropes. The first one is 78 cm. The second one is 39 cm.

How much longer is the first rope compared with the second?

29 cm   39 cm   9 cm   49 cm

○   ○   ○   ○

18. Colour one quarter of these shapes.

19. There is a pattern in these numbers. Write the number that is missing in the box.

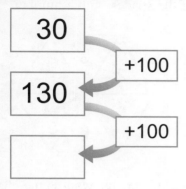

20. Which hand signal should come next in this pattern?

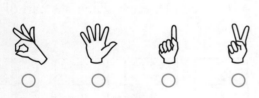

21. Use the table to answer the next question.

Birds in my backyard today

Type of bird	Number of birds
Rosella	3
Magpie	9
Pigeon	16
Galah	2

How many magpies and pigeons are there?

Write your answer here.

22. Here is a shape made up of some blocks.

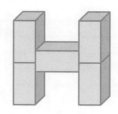

Which one of the four shapes below is the same as the one shown? Is it A, B, C or D?

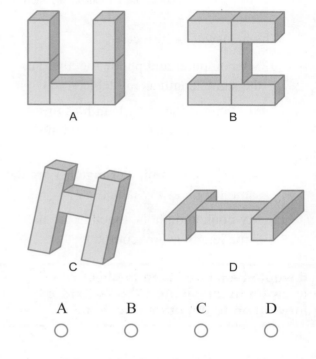

A	B	C	D
○	○	○	○

23. This football costs $3.50.

How much will three footballs cost?

Write your answer here. $

24. This chart shows the length of some objects.

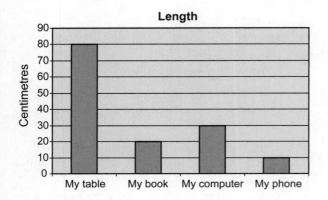

Which answer is correct?

○ My computer and phone together are the same length as my table.

○ My table is the same length as my book, my computer and my phone together.

○ My book and computer together are the same length as my table.

○ My book and phone together are the same length as my computer.

It would be a good idea to check your answers to questions 13 to 24 before moving on to the other questions.

25. Here is a chart showing how many questions were answered correctly in a test.

Patterson	✓✓✓✓✓✓✓✓
Lawson	✓✓✓✓✓
Kendall	✓✓✓✓✓✓✓✓
Gordon	✓✓✓✓✓

Each ✓ stands for one question correct.

How many questions were answered correctly by Gordon?

Write your answer in the box.

26. Who answered the most questions correctly?

Patterson   Lawson   Kendall   Gordon
○   ○   ○   ○

27. There are six spaces that have a number. We can spin the arrow and it will land on one of the spaces with a number.

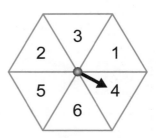

If I spin this arrow, what is the chance it will land on the space for the number 5?

○ 1 out of 6 chances

○ 4 out of 6 chances

○ 6 out of 1 chances

○ 5 out of 6 chances

28. There are four shapes. They are called A, B, C and D. Each shape has part of it coloured.

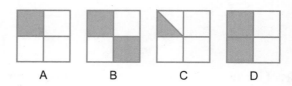

Which shape is one-quarter coloured?

A   B   C   D
○   ○   ○   ○

29. Here is a shape made from different pieces. How many of the pieces are triangular prisms?

2   4   9   6

○   ○   ○   ○

30. There are 18 dollars to be divided. Fred will get twice as much as Jenny.

How much will each person get?

Fred: ☐ dollars

Jenny: ☐ dollars

> **Write your answers in the boxes.**

31. This chart shows a trip taken by John. He passes three buildings.

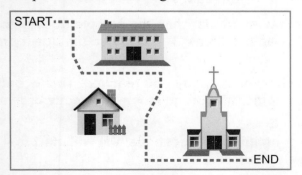

As he passes each building, which one is **NEVER** on John's left-hand side? (Do not include those in front or behind.)

School   House   Church

○   ○   ○

32. There is a car in the middle lane on a freeway. There are 20 cars ahead and 40 cars behind. In the left lane there are 30 cars and in the right lane there are 80 cars.

How many cars are there on this freeway? (Give the closest answer.)

160   165   170   175

○   ○   ○   ○

33. Here is a column of five numbers, starting with 1, then 3, then 5, then 7 and then 9. There is a pattern in these numbers. In the last column draw the dots which finish the pattern.

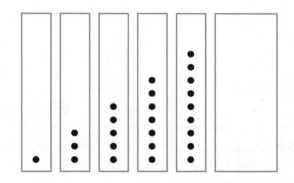

> **Draw your answer in the box.**

34. In this map there are three pathways towards 100.

The three paths start with 20.

Which pathway — A, B or C — will give you exactly 100?

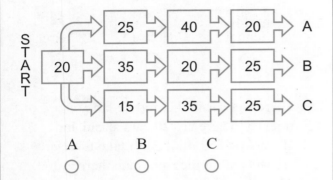

    A   B   C

    ○   ○   ○

35. Here are four fractions.

$$\frac{1}{4} \qquad \frac{1}{2} \qquad \frac{3}{4} \qquad \frac{1}{3}$$

If you take a half of one of them, you will find that it is a quarter. What is the fraction?

$$\frac{1}{4} \qquad \frac{1}{2} \qquad \frac{3}{4} \qquad \frac{1}{3}$$

  ○   ○   ○   ○

36. Here is a puzzle. Find the two missing numbers in this diamond puzzle. Follow the arrows to find the answers.

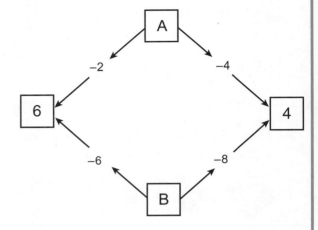

A = 8 B = 12   A = 6 B = 8

    ○   ○

A = 16 B = 8   A = 7 B = 9

    ○   ○

END OF TEST

Well done! You have completed the first Numeracy Test. Even if you don't practise any others, at least you will have done a fair sample of the questions.

How did you go with these test questions? Some were harder than the sample questions. Check to see where you did well and where you had problems. Try to revise the questions that were hard for you.

Use the diagnostic chart on page 30 to see which level of ability you reached. This is only an estimate. Don't be surprised if you answered some difficult questions correctly or even missed some easier questions.

There are now three more practice tests, each containing 36 questions. We will start to include new types of questions in each of these tests.

Check the answers

As you check the answer for each question, mark it as correct (✓) or incorrect (✗). Mark any questions that you omitted or left out as incorrect (✗) for the moment.

Then look at how many you answered correctly in each level. Your level of ability is the point where you started having consistent difficulty with questions. For example, if you answer most questions correctly up to the Intermediate level and then get most questions wrong from then onwards, it is likely your ability is at an Intermediate level. You can ask your parents or your teacher to help you do this if it isn't clear.

We expect you to miss some easy questions and also to answer some hard questions correctly, but your ability level should be where you are starting to find the questions too hard. Some students will reach the top band— this means that their ability cannot be measured by these questions or even the NAPLAN Tests. They found it far too easy.

Understanding the different levels

We have divided the questions into three levels of difficulty:

- Standard
- Intermediate
- Advanced.

For each question we have described the skill involved in answering the question. Then, depending on what sort of skill is involved, we have placed it into one of the three levels. It should make sense, especially when you go back and look at the type of question. The Standard level includes the easiest tasks and then they increase in difficulty.

Don't worry about the level of ability in which you are located. We expect students to be spread across all of the three bands. Also numeracy may or may not be your strongest subject.

The purpose of these practice tests is to help you be as confident as possible and perform to the best of your ability. The purpose of the NAPLAN Tests is to show what you know or can do. For the first time it allows the user to estimate his or her level of ability before taking the actual test and also to see if there is any improvement across the practice tests.

Remember that the levels of ability are only a rough guide. No claim is made that they are perfect. They are only an indicator. Your level might change as you do each practice test. We hope that these brief notes are of some help.

An important note about the NAPLAN Online tests

The NAPLAN Online Numeracy test will be divided into different sections. Students will only have one opportunity to check their answers at the end of each section before proceeding to the next one. This means that after students have completed a section and moved onto the next they will not be able to check their work again. We have included reminders for students to check their work at specific points in the practice tests from now on so they become familiar with this process.

Instructions

As you check the answer for each question, mark it as correct (✓) or incorrect (✗). Mark any questions that you omitted or left out as incorrect (✗) for the moment.

Then look at how many you answered correctly in each level. You will be able to see what level you are at by finding the point where you started having consistent difficulty with questions at a certain level. For example, if you answer most questions correctly up to the Intermediate level and then get most questions wrong from then onwards, it is likely your ability is at the Intermediate level. You can ask your parents or your teacher to help you do this if it isn't clear to you.

Am I able to ...

	SKILL	ESTIMATED LEVEL	✓ or ✗
1	Write a two-digit number to match the number of objects?	Standard	
2	Apply knowledge of place value to compare three-digit numbers?	Standard	
3	Compare the length of objects by observation?	Standard	
4	Name common three dimensional objects?	Standard	
5	Visualise the symmetry of a folded shape?	Standard	
6	Calculate the total value of a set of coins?	Standard	
7	Form equal groups using a diagram showing a collection of objects?	Standard	
8	Locate data in simple and two-way tables?	Standard	
9	Compare the size of different angles by observation?	Standard	
10	Locate position by following simple directions or by using coordinates on a grid?	Standard	
11	Complete a number sentence involving multiplication?	Intermediate	
12	Find an earlier date?	Intermediate	
13	Convert digital time to analogue time?	Intermediate	
14	Use informal units to measure the area of a grid?	Intermediate	
15	Find the number of weeks from a calendar?	Intermediate	
16	Recognise a figure after it has been flipped?	Intermediate	
17	Solve a problem involving the difference between numbers less than 100?	Intermediate	
18	Understand the term *quarters* and use simple fractions?	Intermediate	
19	Continue a number pattern involving counting on by hundreds?	Intermediate	
20	Identify a sequence?	Intermediate	
21	Interpret data in simple tables?	Intermediate	
22	Recognise a model viewed from a different perspective?	Intermediate	
23	Solve everyday money problems involving addition or multiplication?	Advanced	
24	Interpret data from column graphs to confirm a statement?	Advanced	
25	Use a key to interpret picture graphs?	Advanced	
26	Use a key to interpret picture graphs?	Advanced	
27	Use chance terms to describe the outcome in a simple experiment?	Advanced	
28	Use informal units to compare different models?	Advanced	
29	Identify prisms within a composite model?	Advanced	
30	Solve a division problem involving unequal shares?	Advanced	
31	Use a diagram to determine the right-hand side of a journey?	Advanced	
32	Use an appropriate problem-solving strategy such as guess-and-check?	Advanced	
33	Solve a problem?	Intermediate	
34	Follow a numerical pathway?	Advanced	
35	Solve a fraction problem?	Advanced	
36	Solve dual subtraction problems?	Advanced	
	TOTAL		

This is the second Numeracy Test. There are 36 questions.

If you aren't sure what to do, ask your teacher or your parents to help you. Don't be afraid to ask if it isn't clear to you.

Allow around 45 minutes for this test.

Write your answer in the box or colour in the circle with the correct answer. Colour in only one circle for each answer.

1. Here are some bundles of sticks. There are 10 sticks in the bundle.

   There are also some sticks that are not in a bundle.

   Count the sticks. Then write how many TENS and ONES there are altogether.

   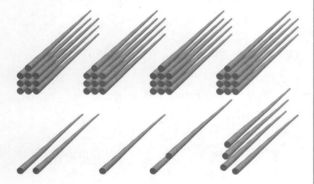

   How many sticks are there altogether?

   Write your answer in the box.

2. What part or fraction of this shape is coloured?

   Did you colour in one of the circles?

   $\frac{3}{4}$ ○ $\frac{1}{4}$ ○ $\frac{1}{2}$ ○

3. When we estimate, we guess the answer. We might say how much or how many we think.

   Using this picture, estimate the number of stars in the sky.

   ○ It is 3.
   ○ It is more than 10.
   ○ It is 5.
   ○ It is 10.

4. Which group of coins can I use to make 35 cents?

   ○   ○   ○

5. I cut this white shape out of the orange paper. Then I folded the paper in half.

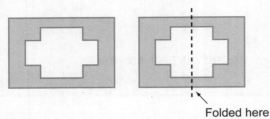

Folded here

Which shape should I see?

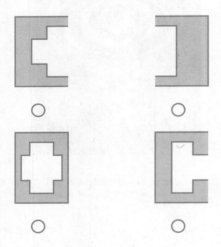

○   ○

○   ○

6. Look at the crayons.

The first child has five crayons.

The next child has nine crayons.

Which sum shows how many crayons there are altogether?

○ 5 + 9 = 13

○ 9 − 5 = 14

○ 14 − 5 = 9

○ 5 + 9 = 14

7. Look at this calendar.

JUNE						
M	**T**	**W**	**T**	**F**	**S**	**S**
1	2	3	4	5	6	7
8	9	10	11	12	13	14
15	16	17	18	19	20	21
22	23	24	25	26	27	28
29	30					

Today is Monday. Next Monday is 22 June. What is the date today?

1 June   8 June   15 June   22 June

○   ○   ○   ○

8. This table shows the score at the end of a game.

Team	Number of points
Red	15
Blue	4
Green	5
Yellow	3
White	12

How many more points did the red team score than the yellow team?

10   11   12   13

○   ○   ○   ○

9. Here are four angles. The angle is shown with a dot. Which is the largest angle?

○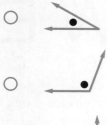

○

○

○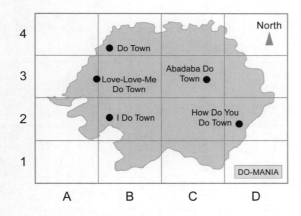

10. Here is a chart. It shows four pictures at different spots in the chart. The map is divided into sections marked 1, 2, 3 and 4 along the side and A, B, C and D along the bottom.

Which town is in D2?

○ I Do Town

○ Love-Love-Me Do Town

○ Do Town

○ How Do You Do Town

11. Here is a piece of wood. It is to be cut into pieces that are 10 centimetres long. How many 10-centimetre pieces can be made from it?

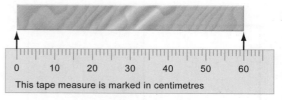

This tape measure is marked in centimetres

Fill in the number sentence below to show how many pieces.

[   ] ÷ 10 = [   ] pieces

Write your answers in these boxes.

12. Here is a block that is made up of separate cubes.

Which sum shows how to find the number of cubes?

○ 3 + 3 + 3   ○ 9 + 9 + 9

○ 9 + 9   ○ 9 × 9 × 9

It would be a good idea to check your answers to questions 1 to 12 before moving on to the other questions.

13. It is morning. Which clock shows the latest time in the morning?

○   ○   ○   ○

14. Here is a pattern made up of hexagons (these are the shapes with six sides).

There is a rectangle in the corner with a black border.

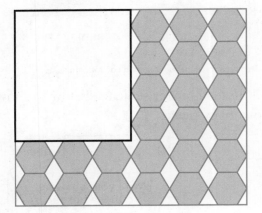

How many hexagons are needed to fill the rectangle? (Hint: use the hexagons that are outside to help you.)

[ ] hexagons

Write your answer in the box.

15. Name the shapes in this figure.

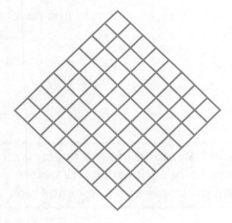

○ They are all rectangles.
○ They are all triangles.
○ They are all squares.
○ They are all cubes.

16. Which of these letters will look the same if it is flipped horizontally or turned over sideways?

P   Q   W   E
○   ○   ○   ○

17. Each boy has drawn some circles. Look at the number of circles drawn by each.

Bob

Ian

Ian has drawn fewer than Bob. How many fewer?

18   22   25   27
○   ○   ○   ○

18. Here are some shapes. Colour one third of these shapes.

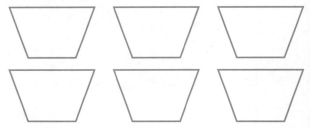

19. There is a pattern in these numbers. Write in the number that is missing.

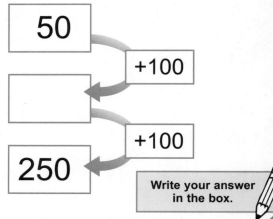

Write your answer in the box.

20. What shape should come next in this pattern?

○   ○   ○   ○

21. Here is a chart of some small countries. It shows their coastline and how long it is.

Country	Coast
Bosnia	20 km
Jordan	26 km
Monaco	4 km
Nauru	30 km
Tuvalu	24 km

Which country has the shortest coastline?

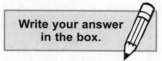

Write your answer in the box.

22. John can walk one kilometre in 10 minutes. How long would it take him to walk around the coastline of Monaco?

○ 30 minutes

○ 40 minutes

○ 50 minutes

○ 60 minutes

23. Here is a shape made out of some blocks.

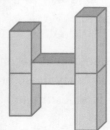

Which one of the four shapes below is the same as the one shown? Is it A, B, C or D?

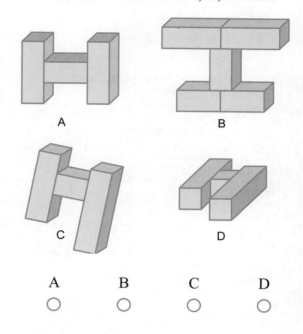

A   B   C   D

○   ○   ○   ○

24. We can flip, slide or turn shapes.

Here is an example. Look closely at what happens to the coloured shape.

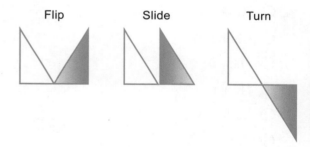

Have we done a flip, a slide or a turn with this coloured shape?

Flip   Slide   Turn

○   ○   ○

It would be a good idea to check your answers to questions 13 to 24 before moving on to the other questions.

25. This table shows the temperature at 2 pm on 25 November one year throughout Australia.

It shows the temperature now. It also shows the forecast highest temperature (or likely temperature) for the day.

City	Temperature Now	Forecast highest temperature for the day
Adelaide	28 °C	26 °C
Brisbane	27 °C	28 °C
Canberra	19 °C	20 °C
Darwin	34 °C	35 °C
Hobart	13 °C	16 °C
Melbourne	23 °C	25 °C
Perth	21 °C	22 °C
Sydney	20 °C	20 °C

Which city is the coldest now?

○ Adelaide

○ Brisbane

○ Canberra

○ Darwin

○ Hobart

○ Melbourne

○ Perth

○ Sydney

26. Which statement is true?

○ The temperature in Adelaide is now more than the forecast high for the day.

○ The temperature in Darwin is now at its forecast highest for the day.

○ The temperature in Sydney and Melbourne is now the same.

○ The temperature in Sydney and Canberra is now the same.

27. This table shows the Hindu calendar. It is used for religious festivals.

The table shows the Hindu Month and the number of days in that month.

It also shows when that month begins in our calendar.

Hindu Calendar

Months	Days	Our date which is the first day of the Hindu month
Chaitra	30	22 March
Vaisakha	31	21 April
Jyaistha	31	22 May
Asadha	31	22 June
Sravana	31	23 July
Bhadrapada	31	23 August
Asvina	30	23 September
Karttika	30	23 October
Margasirsa	30	22 November
Pausa	30	22 December
Magha	30	21 January
Phalguna	30	20 February

I was born on 26 October. In which Hindu month is my birthday?

Write your answer here. ▭

28. An estimate is a guess. For the sum $11 + 7$ an estimate would be around 20.

Why did we pick 20? We sort of guessed.

We changed each number to the closest 10.

11 is closer to 10 than 20 so it becomes 10.

7 is closer to 10 than 0, so it also becomes 10.

The sum is then $10 + 10 = 20$.

Of course the correct answer is 18, but a rough guess is 20. It is fairly close but not perfectly accurate. It is an estimate.

Now estimate the answer to this sum:

31 + 28 = ?

40	50	60	70
○	○	○	○

29. There are three rows. On each row there are some glasses.

Row	Objects
Top	
Middle	
Bottom	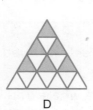

On which row (Top, Middle or Bottom) would I have the best chance of picking the glasses?

○ Top

○ Middle

○ Bottom

30. There are four shapes. They are labelled A, B, C and D. Each shape has part of it coloured.

A   B

C   D

Which shape is coloured one quarter?

A	B	C	D
○	○	○	○

31. A 2-digit number is any number from 10 right up to 99. Draw a circle around the 2-digit multiples of 5.

10	11	12	13	14	15	16	17	18	19
20	21	22	23	24	25	26	27	28	29
30	31	32	33	34	35	36	37	38	39
40	41	42	43	44	45	46	47	48	49
50	51	52	53	54	55	56	57	58	59
60	61	62	63	64	65	66	67	68	69
70	71	72	73	74	75	76	77	78	79
80	81	82	83	84	85	86	87	88	89
90	91	92	93	94	95	96	97	98	99

How many 2-digit multiples of five are there in this table?

Write your answer here.

32. The scores on a dice are shown on the faces. They can be any number from 1 to 6.

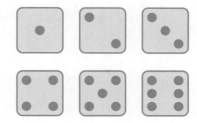

If you throw a dice, which statement is true?

○ It is more likely you will score a 1, 2 or 3.

○ It is more likely you will throw a 6.

○ Any number from 1 to 6 is possible.

○ It is more likely you will score a 4, 5 or 6.

33. This triangle is made up of numbers from 1 to 6. Some numbers have been filled in for you.

When you add the three numbers on each side then each of the three sides of this triangle equals 11.

Write the numbers 1, 2 and 3 in the correct circles.

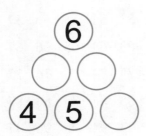

34. There are three pathways towards 100. The three paths start with 8. Which pathway — A, B or C — will give you exactly 100?

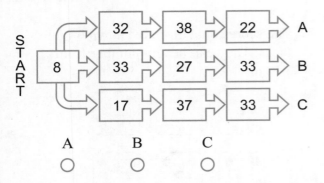

A ○   B ○   C ○

35. Some children catch this bus to school.

At the first stop 8 get on.

At the second stop 7 get on and 3 get off.

At the third stop half get off.

How many children are still on the bus?

5	6	7	8
○	○	○	○

36. Here is a puzzle. You start with a number. You double it. You then add 8. The number you then come up with is 24. What was the first number?

8	7	6	4
○	○	○	○

END OF TEST

Well done! You have completed the second Numeracy Test. We tried to change the questions and some were a little harder.

How did you go with these test questions? Check to see where you did well and where you had problems. Try to revise the questions that were hard for you.

Use the diagnostic chart on page 39 to see which level of ability you reached. This is only an estimate. Don't be surprised if you answered some difficult questions correctly or even missed some easier questions.

There are now two more practice tests, each containing 36 questions. We have included some new types of questions in this test.

Instructions

As you check the answer for each question, mark it as correct (✓) or incorrect (✗). Mark any questions that you omitted or left out as incorrect (✗) for the moment.

Then look at how many you answered correctly in each level. You will be able to see what level you are at by finding the point where you started having consistent difficulty with questions at a certain level. For example, if you answer most questions correctly up to the Intermediate level and then get most questions wrong from then onwards, it is likely your ability is at the Intermediate level. You can ask your parents or your teacher to help you do this if it isn't clear to you.

Am I able to ...

	SKILL	ESTIMATED LEVEL	✓ or ✗
1	Write a two-digit number to match the number of objects?	Standard	
2	Find half of a whole figure?	Standard	
3	Estimate a familiar quantity?	Standard	
4	Calculate the value of some coins?	Standard	
5	Visualise the symmetry of a folded shape?	Standard	
6	Calculate a two-digit addition?	Standard	
7	Locate a date in a calendar?	Standard	
8	Locate data in a simple table and subtract?	Standard	
9	Compare the size of different angles by observation?	Standard	
10	Locate position by following simple directions or by using coordinates on a grid?	Standard	
11	Complete a number sentence involving division?	Intermediate	
12	Use a sum to find the volume of a shape?	Intermediate	
13	Know latest analogue time in terms of am?	Intermediate	
14	Use informal units to measure the area of a grid?	Intermediate	
15	Identify common shapes within a geometric design?	Intermediate	
16	Recognise a figure after it has been flipped?	Intermediate	
17	Solve a problem involving the difference between numbers less than 100?	Intermediate	
18	Understand the term *thirds* and use simple fractions?	Intermediate	
19	Continue a number pattern involving counting on by hundreds?	Intermediate	
20	Identify a sequence?	Intermediate	
21	Interpret data in simple tables?	Intermediate	
22	Use multiplication to solve a problem?	Intermediate	
23	Recognise a model viewed from a different perspective?	Intermediate	
24	Recognise the property of a shape that has been flipped or turned?	Advanced	
25	Interpret data from a chart?	Advanced	
26	Interpret data from a chart to confirm a statement?	Advanced	
27	Select data from a chart to find a date?	Advanced	
28	Use an estimate to describe the outcome?	Advanced	
29	Estimate the chances of selecting an object?	Advanced	
30	Find the fraction of a shape that is coloured?	Advanced	
31	Find two-digit multiples up to 100?	Advanced	
32	Calculate the likelihood of an event?	Advanced	
33	Solve an incomplete problem?	Advanced	
34	Follow a numerical pathway?	Advanced	
35	Solve a problem with a series of steps in calculations?	Advanced	
36	Solve arithmetic puzzle invoving multiplication and addition?	Advanced	
	TOTAL		

This is the third Numeracy Test. There are 36 questions.

If you aren't sure what to do, ask your teacher or your parents to help you.
Don't be afraid to ask if it isn't clear to you.

Allow around 45 minutes for this test.

Write the answer in the box or colour in the circle with the correct answer.
Colour in only one circle for each answer.

1. This drawing shows the number 236.
There are 2 hundreds, 3 tens and 6 units.

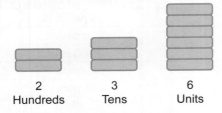

2	3	6
Hundreds	Tens	Units

Now, what number is shown by this drawing?

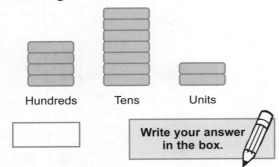

Hundreds   Tens   Units

Write your answer in the box.

2. Each candle shows a birthday in a month.

January   February   March

April   May   June

July   August   September

October   November   December

How many birthdays were there in August?

4	5	6	7
○	○	○	○

3. Look at the shapes in this picture.

Which three different types of shapes are used in this picture?

○ circle, triangle, square

○ circle, triangle, rectangle

○ circle, square, rectangle

○ sphere, cube, triangle

4. Which group of coins can I use to make $1.75?

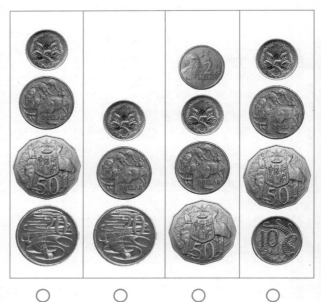

○   ○   ○   ○

5. I cut this white shape out of the orange paper. Then I folded the paper in half.

 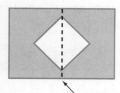

Folded here

Which shape should I see? (This is not drawn to scale.)

   ○      ○

   ○   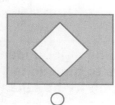   ○

6. Look at the trees. Each has six pieces of fruit on it.

Which sum shows how many pieces of fruit there are altogether?

- ○ 6 + 6 + 6 + 6 = 24
- ○ 6 + 6 + 6 + 6 + 6 = 30
- ○ 6 + 6 + 6 + 6 + 6 + 6 = 36
- ○ 6 + 6 + 6 + 6 + 6 + 6 + 6 = 42

7. Here are some hats.

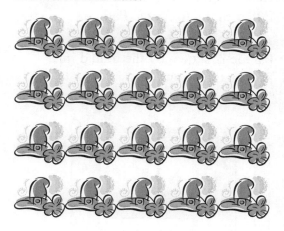

Share them into three equal groups. How many are left over?

4	3	2	1
○	○	○	○

8. This table shows the weight of some parts of a body.

Body Part	Weight (grams)
Brain	1400
Lungs	600
Heart	300
Skin	11000
Kidney	150

Which is the third heaviest body part?

Brain	Lungs	Heart	Kidney
○	○	○	○

9. Which angle is a right angle? A right angle is like the corner of a square. The angle is shown with a dot.

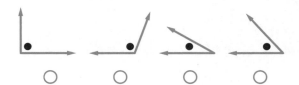

○   ○   ○   ○

10. Here is a map. It shows the path from Edgar Street to Anzac Parade.

The path from Edgar Street to Anzac Parade is shown by the dotted line. Follow the arrow.

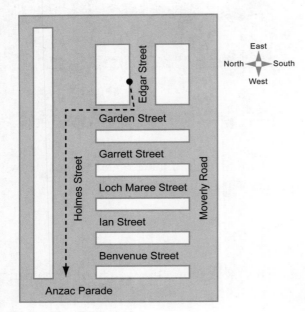

Which streets lead all the way from Edgar Street to Anzac Parade?

○ Garden Street then Holmes Street

○ Garden Street then Garrett Street

○ Garrett Street then Loch Maree Street then Ian Street then Benvenue Street

○ Edgar Street then Holmes Street

11. Is Anzac Parade North, South, East or West of Edgar Street? Use the directions on the side of the map to help you.

North   South   East   West

○   ○   ○   ○

12. Here is a piece of wood. It is to be cut into pieces that are 5 centimetres long. How many 5 centimetre pieces can be cut from it?

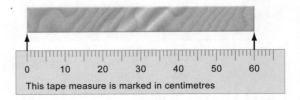

Fill in the number sentence below to show how many pieces.

☐ ÷ 5 = ☐ pieces

> **Write your answers in these boxes.**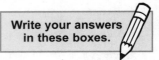

> **It would be a good idea to check your answers to questions 1 to 12 before moving on to the other questions.**

13. Which clock shows the time around 7:30?

○   ○   ○   ○

14. Here is a house. There is a measuring tape underneath. Use this to find the width of the picture.

This tape is marked in metres.

How wide is it?

○ 10 metres   ○ 15 metres

○ 20 metres   ○ 25 metres

15. Name the shapes in this figure.

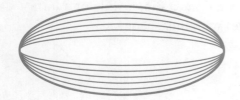

- ◯ They are all circles.
- ◯ They are all spheres.
- ◯ They are all ellipses.
- ◯ They are all rectangles.

16. Which of these letters will look the same if it is flipped horizontally or turned over sideways?

F　　**P**　　**H**　　**J**

　◯　　　◯　　　◯　　　◯

17. To make a bunch of roses you need six flowers.

Look at the roses in the drawings below.

How many bunches can be made?

　5　　　7　　　4　　　6
　◯　　　◯　　　◯　　　◯

18. Here are some shapes. Colour one half of these shapes.

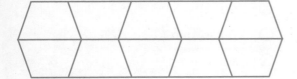

19. There is a pattern in these numbers. Write in the number that is missing.

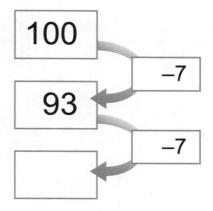

20. Which shape should come next in this pattern?

　◯　　　◯　　　◯　　　◯

21. Here is a chart of energy used by different appliances. This is counted in watts.

Appliance	Energy used
Dishwasher	2000 watts
Computer	400 watts
Printer	350 watts
Light bulb	100 watts
TV	250 watts

Which appliance has the second lowest usage of watts?

Computer　　TV　　Printer　　Light bulb
　◯　　　◯　　　◯　　　◯

22. How many of these money notes are worth twice as much as one of the other notes?

2	3	4	5
○	○	○	○

23. Here is a shape made out of some blocks.

Which one of the four shapes below is the same as the one shown? Is it A, B, C or D?

A

B

C   D

A	B	C	D
○	○	○	○

24. We can flip, slide or turn shapes.

Have we done a flip, a slide or a turn (rotate) with this shape?

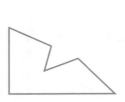 

Flip	Slide	Turn
○	○	○

> **It would be a good idea to check your answers to questions 13 to 24 before moving on to the other questions.**

25. This table shows some wars. It shows when they started and when they finished. At the time of writing, some are still going.

Years	War
1914–1918	World War 1
1939–1945	World War 2
1950–1953	Korean War
1957–1975	Vietnam War
1991	Gulf War
2001–	Afghanistan – War on Terror
2003–	Iraqi War

Which is the shortest war?

○ World War 1

○ World War 2

○ Korean War

○ Vietnam War

○ Gulf War

○ Afghanistan

○ Iraqi War

26. Which statement is true?

○ The war in Afghanistan is longer than World War 2.

○ The Korean War was shorter than the Gulf War.

○ The Vietnam War was before the Korean War.

○ World War 2 has not finished.

27. The world's largest book costs about $10 000. It is around the size of a very large kitchen table.

Which of these calculations would you do if you wanted to buy 5 of these books for your friends?

○ divide $10 000 by five

○ add five to $10 000

○ subtract five from $10 000

○ multiply $10 000 by five

28. The perimeter is the distance around something. Here is a simple example to remind you how to find the perimeter.

Example

The perimeter of this shape is 6 cm.

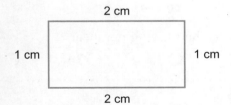

Now estimate the perimeter or the distance around this complicated figure. The distance around each side is shown for you (it is not exact). We do not want the exact answer. We want you to guess or estimate the answer.

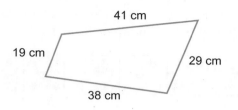

110 cm   120 cm   130 cm   140 cm
  ○   ○   ○   ○

29. Choose the correct statement.

○ There are more odd numbers than even numbers.

○ Some odd numbers can be divided evenly by two.

○ The largest ever odd number is 9 999 999 999 999 999 999 999 999 999 999 999 999.

○ An odd number is an even number plus one.

30. There are signs missing in this calculation. Use a $+$ or $-$ or $\times$ or $\div$, to fill the spaces. The spaces are shown with 3 dots.

$$8 \ldots (6 \ldots 4) = 80$$

> **Write your answers over the sets of 3 dots.**

31. Add any three numbers in a row. It could be $1 + 2 + 3$ or $2 + 3 + 4$ or even $20 + 21 + 22$ or even $98 + 99 + 100$.

Choose the correct statement.

○ The answer to the addition is always an odd number.

○ The answer to the addition is always an even number.

○ The answer to the addition is always a multiple of three.

○ The answer to the addition is always two times the middle number.

32. The scores on a dice are shown on the faces. They can be any number from 1 to 6.

You throw a dice twice and add the scores. The first dice gives a number from 1 to 6. The second dice also gives a number from 1 to 6.

How many different ways can the total of the two thrown dice add up to seven?

3	7	5	6
○	○	○	○

33. This triangle is made up of numbers from 12 to 17. Some numbers have been filled in for you.

When you add the three numbers on each side then each of the three sides of this triangle equals 44.

Write the numbers 12, 13 and 14 in the correct circles.

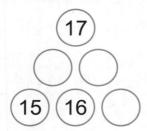

34. There are three pathways towards 100. The three paths start with 200. Which pathway — A, B or C — will give you exactly 100?

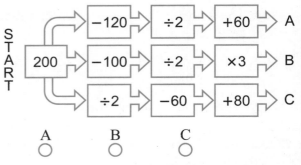

A	B	C
○	○	○

35. Look at the drawing below. There is a pattern but one part is missing. This is shown with a question mark (?).

Pick which piece (A, B, C or D) will complete the pattern.

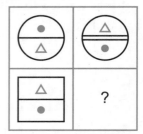

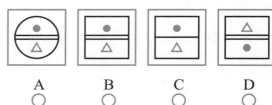

A	B	C	D
○	○	○	○

36. Here are some numbers. There is a pattern in these numbers.

14 21 28 ? 42

What is the missing number?

○ 32   ○ 33   ○ 34   ○ 35

END OF TEST

Well done! You have completed the third Numeracy Test. We tried to change the questions and some were a little harder. Don't worry if you didn't finish it in time as we added some new types of questions.

How did you go with these test questions? Check to see where you did well and where you had problems. Try to revise the questions that were hard for you.

Use the diagnostic chart on page 47 to see which level of ability you reached. This is only an estimate. Don't be surprised if you answered some difficult questions correctly or even missed some easier questions.

There is now one last practice test that contains 36 questions.

Instructions

As you check the answer for each question, mark it as correct (✓) or incorrect (✗). Mark any questions that you omitted or left out as incorrect (✗) for the moment.

Then look at how many you answered correctly in each level. You will be able to see what level you are at by finding the point where you started having consistent difficulty with questions at a certain level. For example, if you answer most questions correctly up to the Intermediate level and then get most questions wrong from then onwards, it is likely your ability is at the Intermediate level. You can ask your parents or your teacher to help you do this if it isn't clear to you.

Am I able to ...

	SKILL	ESTIMATED LEVEL	✓ or ✗
1	Write a three-digit number to match the number of objects?	Standard	
2	Use pictures in a chart?	Standard	
3	Recognise shapes?	Standard	
4	Calculate the value of some coins?	Standard	
5	Visualise the symmetry of a folded shape?	Standard	
6	Calculate an addition?	Standard	
7	Decide the remainder after forming equal groups from a collection of objects?	Standard	
8	Locate data in a simple table?	Standard	
9	Recognise a right angle?	Standard	
10	Locate positions from a map?	Standard	
11	Locate directions from a map?	Intermediate	
12	Complete a number sentence involving division?	Intermediate	
13	Know analogue time?	Intermediate	
14	Find the length from a measuring tape?	Intermediate	
15	Identify common shapes within a geometric design?	Intermediate	
16	Recognise a figure after it has been flipped?	Intermediate	
17	Divide a quantity into groups?	Intermediate	
18	Understand the term *half* and use simple fractions?	Intermediate	
19	Continue a number pattern subtracting seven?	Intermediate	
20	Identify a sequence?	Intermediate	
21	Interpret data in simple tables?	Intermediate	
22	Recognise money that is double in value?	Intermediate	
23	Recognise a model viewed from a different perspective?	Intermediate	
24	Recognise the property of a shape that has been turned?	Advanced	
25	Interpret data from a chart?	Advanced	
26	Interpret data from a chart to confirm a statement?	Advanced	
27	Select a mathematical operation to find an answer?	Advanced	
28	Use an estimate to determine the perimeter?	Advanced	
29	Define an odd number?	Advanced	
30	Insert the signs in a sum?	Advanced	
31	Find a pattern in the sum of consecutive numbers?	Advanced	
32	Calculate the likelihood of an event?	Advanced	
33	Solve an incomplete problem?	Advanced	
34	Follow a numerical pathway?	Advanced	
35	Find the missing part of a matrix?	Advanced	
36	Solve number series based on multiples of seven?	Advanced	
	TOTAL		

This is the fourth Numeracy Test. There are 36 questions.

If you aren't sure what to do, ask your teacher or your parents to help you. Don't be afraid to ask if it isn't clear to you.

These questions will be harder than the earlier Numeracy Tests so don't worry if you can't answer all the questions. Allow around 45 minutes for this test.

Write your answer in the box or colour in the circle with the correct answer. Colour in only one circle for each answer.

1. Here are some drawings. The beads show the number of Hundreds, Tens and Units. Which drawing shows the number 561?

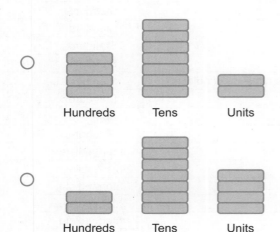

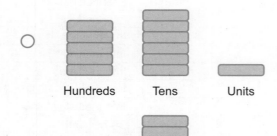

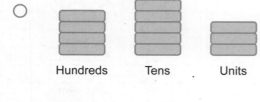

2. Show which is the largest number (not in size but in quantity) in the sequence below.

349 496 694 934

○   ○   ○   ○

3. Write your answer to this calculation.

$$\begin{array}{r} 9 \\ -\ 6 \\ \hline \end{array}$$

4. Write your answer to this calculation.

$$\begin{array}{r} 8 \\ +\ 3 \\ \hline \end{array}$$

5. Write your answer to this calculation.

$$\begin{array}{r} 6 \\ \times\ 2 \\ \hline \end{array}$$

Did you colour in one of the circles?

6. Look at the shapes in this picture.

Which of the following shapes is used?

○ triangle

○ cross

○ rectangle

○ sphere

7. Which group of notes make a total of $85?

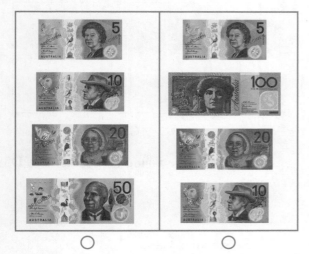

○   ○

○   ○

8. A white space has been cut out of the orange rectangle. Find the two pieces which will fill in the space exactly without being rotated or turned.

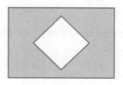

| 1 | 2 | 3 | 4 |

[ ] and [ ]

Write two numbers, one in each of these boxes.

9. Look at the pagodas. Each has five roofs.

Which sum shows how many roofs there are altogether?

○ $4 \times 5 = 24$

○ $5 \times 4 = 9$

○ $4 \times 5 = 25$

○ $4 \times 5 = 20$

10. Here are some numbers.

⓪ ⓪ ① ② ① ②

③ ④ ⑤ ③ ④ ⑤

⑥ ⑦ ⑧ ⑨ ⑥ ⑦ ⑧ ⑨

Put seven in one group and seven in another group. How many are left over?

8   7   6   5

○   ○   ○   ○

11. This table shows the sales of some songs.

Song	Year	Sales
Candle in the Wind	1997	37 million
Hey Jude	1968	10 million
I Want to Hold Your Hand	1963	12 million
It's Now or Never	1960	12 million
Rock Around the Clock	1954	17 million
White Christmas	1945	30 million

Which is the third most popular song?

○ White Christmas

○ Rock Around the Clock

○ It's Now or Never

○ I Want to Hold Your Hand

12. Here is a balance. It is like a scale which weighs two things.

Which statement is true?

○ The right side is heavier than the left.

○ The left side is heavier than the right.

○ Both sides are the same weight.

> It would be a good idea to check your answers to questions 1 to 12 before moving on to the other questions.

13. Here is a chart of a real island. It is called Megisti.

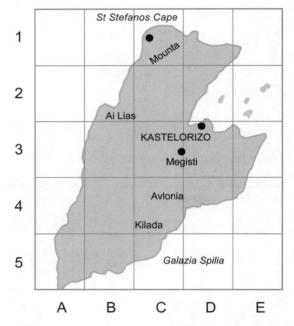

What part of the island is located near D3?

○ Megisti

○ Avlonia

○ St Stefanos Cape

○ Galazia Spilia

14. Which is the furthest distance between two places on this map?

○ Galazia Spilia to Kilada

○ Kilada to Avlonia

○ Megisti to Ai Lias

○ Avlonia to Megisti

15. Here is a picture. It is cut into two pieces.

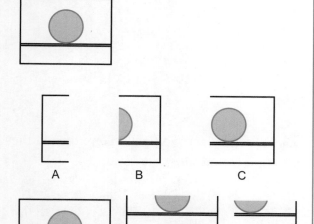

Show the two pieces that make the top picture.

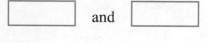

and

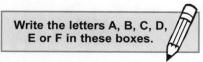

Write the letters A, B, C, D, E or F in these boxes.

16. This clock shows the time now. How many minutes are there before 10:30?

- ○ 90 minutes
- ○ 60 minutes
- ○ 30 minutes
- ○ 5 minutes

17. Here is the corner of a pattern. It is made up of two grey and two white squares.

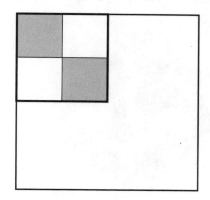

How many squares (grey and white) are needed to fill all the space?

16	12	8	20
○	○	○	○

18. Connect the diamond shapes in this figure. Draw a line which joins all the diamond shapes.

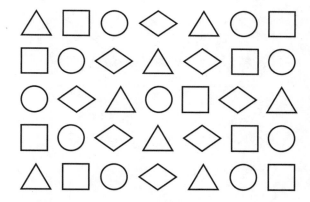

What shape have you drawn?

- ○ It is a circle.
- ○ It is a diamond.
- ○ It is a triangle.

19. Here is a face. It is made up of figures and shapes. The mouth is around 2 centimetres wide.

How wide is the whole of the face?

- ○ 4 centimetres
- ○ 5 centimetres
- ○ 7 centimetres
- ○ 9 centimetres

20. There are three figures. Each contains shapes.

Look at the shapes in these three figures. How are they grouped together?

- ○ by colour
- ○ by type of shape
- ○ by size
- ○ by number

21. Complete this calculation.

$$51$$
$$+\ 27$$

22. Complete this calculation.

$$23$$
$$-\ 15$$

23. How much do you get when you add these money notes together?

$175	$185	$195	$200
○	○	○	○

24. These pictures of clocks are in order. They show a pattern.

Which clock comes next in the pattern?

○ ○ ○ ○

It would be a good idea to check your answers to questions 13 to 24 before moving on to the other questions.

25. There is a pattern in these three shapes.

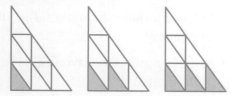

Which one of the four shapes below continues the pattern?

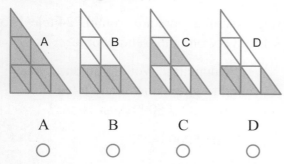

A	B	C	D
○	○	○	○

26. There is a pattern in these numbers. Write the number that is being subtracted.

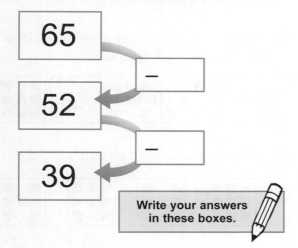

Write your answers in these boxes.

27. We can flip, slide or turn shapes.

Have we done a flip, a slide or a turn (rotate) with this coloured shape?

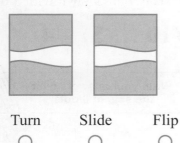

Turn	Slide	Flip
○	○	○

28. Here is a shape made out of some blocks.

Which one of the four shapes below is the same as the one here? Is it A, B, C or D?

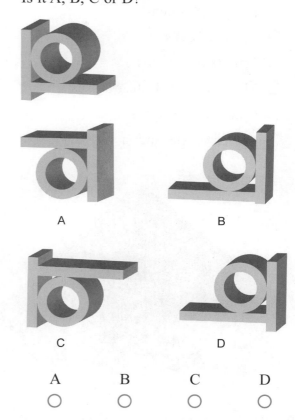

A	B	C	D
○	○	○	○

29. This table shows the seven wonders of the ancient world and when they were built. The dates are not exact. BC means that they are dates Before Christ.

Seven Wonders	Date
Colossus of Rhodes	305 BC
Hanging Gardens of Babylon	600 BC
Mausoleum of Halicarnassus	350 BC
Pharos of Alexandria	279 BC
Statue of Zeus	450 BC
Temple of Artemis	550 BC
The Great Pyramid of Giza	2500 BC

Which was the newest or last of the Seven Wonders of the World?

○ Great Pyramid

○ Hanging Gardens

○ Statue of Zeus

○ Temple of Artemis

○ Mausoleum of Halicarnassus

○ Colossus of Rhodes

○ Pharos of Alexandria

30. The Great Pyramid of Giza is about the size of six football fields. It is the only one of the Seven Wonders of the World to survive. It was built as a burial place for a king. Here is a photo and a drawing of the Pyramid for you. Answer the question about the Pyramid.

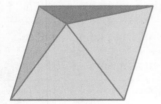

The Pyramid has four sides. Each side is about 230 m long.

Which statement is true?

○ The distance around the pyramid is just over 900 metres.

○ The distance around the pyramid is just over 1000 metres.

○ The distance around the pyramid is 230 metres.

31. In Australia there are around 724 televisions for every one thousand people.

What calculation would you do if you wanted to guess how many televisions were owned by 5000 Australians?

○ divide 5000 by 724

○ add 5000 to 724

○ subtract 724 from 5000

○ multiply 724 by five

32. Here is a pattern of dots in some squares. One part of the pattern is missing.

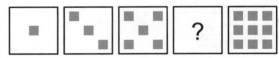

Which is the missing pattern?

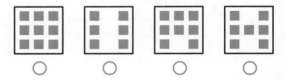

○ ○ ○ ○

33. There are signs missing in this calculation. Use a $+$ or $-$ or $\times$ or $\div$ to fill the spaces. The spaces are shown with 3 dots.

$$20 \ldots (10 \ldots 5) = 4$$

> Write your answers over the sets of 3 dots.

34. Here is a chart of when some inventions were developed.

Invention	Year
Ballpoint pen (biro)	1938
Calculator	1971
Credit card	1950
Crossword puzzle	1913
Ice cream cone	1904
Internet	1989
iPod	2000
Lego	1955
Sliced bread	1928

How many inventions were developed between 1925 and 1950?

5   4   3   2
○   ○   ○   ○

35. How many years between the invention of the ice cream cone and the invention of sliced bread?

29   21   28   24
○   ○   ○   ○

36. Here are three scales. They are balanced. This means that both sides weigh the same.

** _____ ○   □ _____ ○○   ○✦ _____ □
▲   ▲   ▲

Here is another scale. A weight is missing.

? _____ □
▲

Which weight should go there so that it will balance?

○✦✦   **✦○   ✦✦*   **✦
○   ○   ○   ○

END OF TEST

Well done! You have completed the final Numeracy Test. We tried to change the questions and some were a little harder. Don't worry if you didn't finish it in time as we added some new types of questions.

How did you go with these test questions? Check to see where you did well and where you had problems. Try to revise the questions that were hard for you.

Use the diagnostic chart on page 56 to see which level of ability you reached. This is only an estimate. Don't be surprised if you answered some difficult questions correctly or even missed some easier questions.

This is the last Numeracy Test. We will start to look at Literacy tasks in the sections that follow. Now take a well-earned rest.

Instructions

As you check the answer for each question, mark it as correct ($\checkmark$) or incorrect ($\times$). Mark any questions that you omitted or left out as incorrect ($\times$) for the moment.

Then look at how many you answered correctly in each level. You will be able to see what level you are at by finding the point where you started having consistent difficulty with questions at a certain level. For example, if you answer most questions correctly up to the Intermediate level and then get most questions wrong from then onwards, it is likely your ability is at the Intermediate level. You can ask your parents or your teacher to help you do this if it isn't clear to you.

Am I able to ...

	SKILL	ESTIMATED LEVEL	$\checkmark$ or $\times$
1	Use place values to match three-digit numbers?	Standard	
2	Select the highest number?	Standard	
3	Complete a subtraction?	Standard	
4	Complete an addition?	Standard	
5	Complete a multiplication?	Standard	
6	Recognise shapes?	Standard	
7	Calculate the value of some notes?	Standard	
8	Complete a shape?	Standard	
9	Solve a problem using multiplication?	Standard	
10	Decide the remainder after forming equal groups from a collection of objects?	Standard	
11	Locate data in a simple table?	Standard	
12	Compare the weight of different sides by observation?	Intermediate	
13	Locate positions from a map?	Intermediate	
14	Locate distances from a map?	Intermediate	
15	Find the pieces that complete a pattern?	Intermediate	
16	Find the number of minutes before a certain time of day?	Intermediate	
17	Use informal units to measure the area of a grid?	Intermediate	
18	Identify a common shape?	Intermediate	
19	Estimate the length of an object?	Intermediate	
20	Find the basis for grouping shapes?	Intermediate	
21	Complete an addition?	Intermediate	
22	Complete a subtraction?	Intermediate	
23	Add money values?	Intermediate	
24	Identify a sequence?	Intermediate	
25	Complete a pattern in the fraction of a shape that is coloured?	Intermediate	
26	Continue a number pattern subtracting thirteen?	Advanced	
27	Recognise the property of a shape that has been flipped?	Advanced	
28	Recognise a model viewed from a different perspective?	Advanced	
29	Interpret data from a chart?	Advanced	
30	Use data from a table to confirm a statement?	Advanced	
31	Select a mathematical operation to find an answer?	Advanced	
32	Find the missing pattern in a series of numbers?	Advanced	
33	Insert the signs in a sum?	Advanced	
34	Interpret data in simple tables?	Advanced	
35	Refer to a table and subtract numbers?	Advanced	
36	Balance quantities?	Advanced	
	TOTAL		

This is the first Reading Test. There are 39 questions.

If you aren't sure what to do, ask your teacher or your parents to help you. Don't be afraid to ask if it isn't clear to you.

Allow around 45 minutes for this test. Take a short break if necessary.

In this test you will need to look at a picture or read something first. Then read each question and colour in the circle with the correct answer.

Look at the drawing and answer question 1.

From *Art Today*, CD1/0051/QRT096/.JPG

1. What is happening in this drawing?
   - ○ The rabbit is reading the warning from the owner.
   - ○ The rabbit is reading a street sign.
   - ○ The sign is giving directions to rabbits.
   - ○ The rabbit is looking at a sign.

Did you colour in one of the circles?

Read *Solomon Grundy* and answer questions 2 to 5

Solomon Grundy

Solomon Grundy

Born on a Monday

Christened on Tuesday

Married on Wednesday

Took ill on Thursday

Worse on Friday

Died on Saturday

Buried on Sunday

This is the end

Of Solomon Grundy.

2. What type of writing is this?
   - ○ *Solomon Grundy* is a poem.
   - ○ *Solomon Grundy* is a story.
   - ○ *Solomon Grundy* is a book.

3. Who was buried on Sunday?
   - ○ Solomon Grundy
   - ○ his wife
   - ○ the end

4. When was Solomon Grundy married?

○ Sunday ○ Thursday

○ Monday ○ Friday

○ Tuesday ○ Saturday

○ Wednesday

5. *Solomon Grundy* was most likely written for

○ adults.

○ teenagers.

○ children.

Look at the cover of this book and answer question 6.

From *Art Today*, CD1/0036/LIF066.JPG

6. Which sentence is true?

○ It is a fairy tale about a man and a boy.

○ It is about fairies, animals and people.

○ It is a true story about a man and a boy.

○ It is about pets that sing and dance.

Did you colour in one of the circles?

Look at this page from a TV guide and answer questions 7 to 12.

Time	Channel Two	Time	Channel Seven
4.00	Music Videos	5.00	Video Clips
7.00	Worldwatch	7.30	Sunday Sunrise
7.30	Soccer Sunday	8.00	The Sunday Business Show
9.30	Worship Sunday	9.00	Living Life
10.30	Cricket	10.00	The Entertainment Show
12.30	Movie: "The Man who Saved Hollywood" (1976 M rpt) starring Ryan Witherspoon and Marcel Rousseau.	10.30	Masterpiece (rpt)
		11.00	Gardens Galore: with Lou Loudi
		11.30	That's Cooking
		12.00	Wonderful World of Sports
2.30	Surprise, Surprise!	1.00	Formula One Racing
3.00	Travel Today: The Greek Islands with Pamela Thosdromo.	3.00	Movie: "Nine Lives" (1998 PG) starring Peg Ryan and Burt Dussille.
4.00	The Lucy and Cheryl Show (rpt)		
4.30	Tenpin Bowling	5.30	Sunday Chef: with Lee Margos and Troy Kota.
5.00	Ciao!		
6.00	News and Weather	6.00	World News
7.00	The Wildlife Show (rpt)	7.00	World Sport
8.00	Everybody Loves Jerry!	7.30	Home Sweet Home
8.30	Movie: "The Price of Freedom" (1998 M rpt) starring Austin Eleftheri and Victor Mitchell.	8.00	Opera Tonight
		9.00	Movie: "Cruel Interrogation" (1999 MA) starring Lisa Murray, Henry Curley and Miles Tipota.
10.30	Latenight News		
11.30	Soccer: European Champions League	11.30	Sunday Replay: Sport Highlights
1.00	Tennis Highlights	12.30	TV Shopping Direct (rpt)
2.00	Close	1.30	Close

Write your answers on the lines.

7. At what time does Channel Seven end?

_____

8. For which day of the week is this TV guide?

_____

9. How many sporting programs are on Channel Two on this day?

_____

10. List one of the stars in the movie *Cruel Interrogation*.

_____

11. Name one of the news programs on Channel Two.

_____

12. What do you think *rpt* means after the title of a program?

_____

It would be a good idea to check your answers to questions 1 to 12 before moving on to the other questions.

Read *Letter to a Wizard* and answer questions 13 to 16.

Letter to a Wizard

Please let me come

And be a wizard for
the day

How much fun we'd
have,

I'd really love to stay!

Oh how splendid it'll be,

Us wizards, you and me,

We could even make

Some spider cobweb tea!

I'd like to ride your broomstick,

If you just show me how.

I'm sure it's just as easy,

To turn my brother into a cow!

Oh, please Mr Wizard,

I'll wear a big black pointed hat,

And my magic wizard's cloak,

I'll even bring a juicy rat.

Imagine all the spells,

We can create together,

We can turn teachers into toads,

We can even change the weather!

I can be your helper,

I'll work hard all day long,

I'll try my very hardest,

Not to do a single thing wrong!

Love from Monique

13. What is the name of this poem?
- ○ Please let me come
- ○ Anon
- ○ Letter from a Wizard
- ○ Letter to a Wizard

14. What wizard's clothing is mentioned in the poem? (Colour in more than one circle if necessary.)
- ○ belt
- ○ jacket
- ○ magic wand
- ○ black pointy hat
- ○ trousers
- ○ cloak
- ○ broomstick
- ○ rat

15. What is this poem mainly about? Write your answer on the lines.

_____

_____

_____

_____

16. Why does the author want to be a wizard for the day? (Colour in more than one circle if necessary.)
- ○ She thinks it would be fun.
- ○ She needs a job.
- ○ She would like to fly a broomstick.
- ○ She likes eating rats.
- ○ She would like to create spells.
- ○ She wants to be a teacher.

Read *Little Jane and the Poor Man* and answer questions 17 to 20.

Little Jane and the Poor Man

This is Jane Anderson and her sister. They have been out this morning. As they were coming home they saw a poor man lying upon the ground. He was lame and unable to walk. Jane and her sister felt very sorry for him and when they were about to leave they gave him a few pennies which they had in their bags. This was very kind.

They were so willing to part with their pennies that they might enable the old man to buy a loaf of bread or some cake for his dinner.

We should always be ready to supply the needs of the poor. We do not know whether we may become poor some day and also need the help of friends.

Adapted from The Project Gutenberg e-book of *Pleasing stories for good children. By a friend to youth* by Truman and Smith

17. Where would you expect to see this story?
   ○ in a magazine
   ○ in a book
   ○ in a comic
   ○ on the Internet

18. What is the purpose of the story?
   ○ to teach us to help the poor
   ○ to teach us about the olden times
   ○ to teach us how to have fun
   ○ to teach us about poverty

19. What are the *pennies* in the story?
   ○ food
   ○ jewellery
   ○ coins
   ○ vouchers

20. Why does the story say that we should help the poor?
   ○ We should help the poor because they need some bread and cake.
   ○ We should help the poor because we are kind.
   ○ We should help the poor because they are lame and cannot walk.
   ○ We should help the poor because one day we might also need help.

Look at the pictures and answer question 21.

21. Which picture matches the saying *Don't stop the plough to catch a mouse*?

   Colour in one circle.

○ A   ○ B

○ C   ○ D

Adapted from The Project Gutenberg e-book of *Dumpy Proverbs* by C Honor and C Appleton, Grant Richards, 1903

Look at the pictures and answer question 22.

22. Which picture matches the saying *Time and tide wait for no man*?
Colour in one circle.

○ A   ○ B

○ C   ○ D

Adapted from The Project Gutenberg e-book of *Dumpy Proverbs* by C Honor and C Appleton, Grant Richards, 1903

Look at the pictures and answer question 23.

23. Which picture matches the saying *It is an ill wind that blows nobody any good*?
Colour in one circle.

○ A   ○ B

○ C   ○ D

Adapted from The Project Gutenberg e-book of *Dumpy Proverbs* by C Honor and C Appleton, Grant Richards, 1903

It would be a good idea to check your answers to questions 13 to 23 before moving on to the other questions.

Read the words from a popular song and answer questions 24 to 29.

BLUE (da ba dee)

Yo listen up here's a story about a little guy that lives in a blue world and all day and all night and everything he sees is just blue like him inside and outside, blue; his house with a blue little window and a blue Corvette and everything is blue for him and his self and everybody around 'cause he ain't got nobody to listen …

Lyrics taken from 'Blue (da ba dee)' by Eiffel 65

24. What is the name of this song?
   ○ Blue
   ○ Blue (da ba dee)
   ○ Story about a little guy that lives in a blue world

25. What is this song about?
   ○ It is a song about a little man that lives in a blue world.
   ○ It is a song about a little man that lives all day and all night.
   ○ It is a song about everything a man sees.

26. Which sentence is true?
   ○ Everything he sees is blue.
   ○ He sees inside and outside.
   ○ He sees everybody blue.

27. What are some of the things that he sees?
   ○ the inside and outside
   ○ the inside, his house, the window
   ○ his house, the window, a Corvette

28. Why is the man unhappy?

○ because everything he has is blue

○ because he has a blue home

○ because there is no-one to talk to

29. In the song the word *Yo* could mean different things. In this song it could mean

○ Hi.   ○ yesterday.

○ good.   ○ young man.

Read the passage and answer questions 30 to 39.

The first Olympic Games were held in 776 BC and were dedicated to Zeus, the greatest of all gods. They were held every four years in Olympia, Greece. All Greek citizens were invited to attend and compete, but there was a strict ban on women.

To begin with the festival lasted a single day, but later this increased to five days. On the first day there were sacrifices to the gods and then the events began. The first events were the *diaulus* (a foot race two lengths of the stadium), then later running, wrestling, jumping, discus, javelin, boxing and the most exciting of all—the chariot races. The prize for the winners of the first Olympics was a wreath made of an olive tree branch and sums of money.

How different these Olympics were to those of today! Now people all over the world watch to see their country compete in a spirit of friendship. They are held in different nations and not in ancient Olympia. Now men and women compete. Greece hosted the Olympic Games when they were held in Athens in 2004 and Beijing hosted the games in 2008.

30. In what year were the first Olympic games held?

○ 776 BC

○ 2004

○ 2008

31. Who is named as a god?

○ Zeus

○ Olympia

○ diaulus

32. In which city were the Olympics held in 2004?

○ Greece

○ Beijing

○ Athens

33. The ancient Olympics [more than one answer is correct]

○ were held every four years.

○ allowed both men and women to compete.

○ invited all Greek citizens to compete.

34. What is the author's purpose?

○ The purpose of the text is to inform.

○ The purpose of the text is to persuade.

○ The purpose of the text is to entertain.

○ The purpose of the text is to advertise.

35. What is the purpose of the first paragraph?

○ It is an introduction to Athens, Greece.

○ It provides a conclusion to Sydney, Australia.

○ It begins the story of the Olympics.

○ It aims to connect Sydney and Beijing.

36. Which statement about the first Olympics is false?

- ○ The prize was a wreath made of an olive branch.
- ○ The games were dedicated to the god Zeus.
- ○ The Olympics were held every four years.
- ○ All Greeks were invited to attend and participate.

37. What does the word *sacrifice* mean?

- ○ remove
- ○ complete
- ○ offering
- ○ eliminate

38. To begin with, how long did the festival last for?

- ○ 1 day
- ○ 5 days
- ○ 4 years
- ○ 2 days

39. What is a *diaulus*?

- ○ a disease
- ○ an Ancient Greek god
- ○ a type of race
- ○ a city in Greece

END OF TEST

Well done! You have completed the first Reading Test. This test had different types of questions. They are like comprehension passages. You had to look at something or read something and then make a judgement.

How did you find these questions? We hope that you found them interesting. There are further questions in the next Reading Test. The next test contains some different questions. Take a long break before doing any more tests!

Use the diagnostic chart on page 64 to see which level of ability you reached. This is only an estimate. Don't be surprised if you answered some difficult questions correctly or even missed some easier questions.

Please note that multiple interpretations are possible for the levels of difficulty of these tasks. Also, some questions involve skills from different levels. This is only an initial guide to the approximate level of the reading skill assessed.

An important note about the NAPLAN Online tests

The NAPLAN Online Reading test will be divided into different sections. Students will only have one opportunity to check their answers at the end of each section before proceeding to the next one. This means that after students have completed a section and moved onto the next they will not be able to check their work again. We have included reminders for students to check their work at specific points in the practice tests from now on so they become familiar with this process.

Instructions

As you check the answer for each question, mark it as correct (✓) or incorrect (✗). Mark any questions that you omitted or left out as incorrect (✗) for the moment.

Then look at how many you answered correctly in each level. You will be able to see what level you are at by finding the point where you started having consistent difficulty with questions at a certain level. For example, if you answer most questions correctly up to the Intermediate level and then get most questions wrong from then onwards, it is likely your ability is at the Intermediate level. You can ask your parents or your teacher to help you do this if it isn't clear to you.

Am I able to ...

	SKILL	ESTIMATED LEVEL	✓ or ✗
1	Make some meaning from a picture?	Standard	
2	Describe the type of text?	Standard	
3	Make some meaning from short texts that have simple sentences?	Standard	
4	Make some meaning from short texts that have simple sentences?	Standard	
5	Describes the audience for a text?	Standard	
6	Make some meaning from a picture?	Standard	
7	Find clearly stated information?	Standard	
8	Make connections between pieces of clearly stated information?	Standard	
9	Find clearly stated information?	Standard	
10	Make connections between pieces of clearly stated information?	Standard	
11	Interpret information?	Intermediate	
12	Identify meaning of words from their context?	Intermediate	
13	Find clearly stated information?	Standard	
14	Make connections between pieces of clearly stated information?	Standard	
15	Identify the meaning?	Standard	
16	Identify the main idea?	Intermediate	
17	Infer the source of a passage?	Intermediate	
18	Find the purpose of a story?	Intermediate	
19	Define a word that is not in common use?	Intermediate	
20	Find the meaning of a story?	Intermediate	
21	Match a picture to a saying?	Intermediate	
22	Match a picture to a saying?	Intermediate	
23	Match a picture to a saying?	Intermediate	
24	Identify the title?	Standard	
25	Identify the story of the song?	Advanced	
26	Identify a common idea?	Advanced	
27	Connect information?	Intermediate	
28	Draw a conclusion?	Advanced	
29	Identify an expression in a song?	Advanced	
30	Identify a date from a text?	Standard	
31	Find a name in a text?	Standard	
32	Select the name of a city in a text?	Intermediate	
33	Select information?	Advanced	
34	Infer the purpose?	Advanced	
35	Recognise the purpose of the opening paragraph?	Advanced	
36	Connect ideas?	Intermediate	
37	Identify the meaning of a word?	Intermediate	
38	Locate information?	Intermediate	
39	Identify a word?	Advanced	
	TOTAL		

READING TEST 2

This is the second Reading Test. There are 39 questions.

If you aren't sure what to do, ask your teacher or your parents to help you.
Don't be afraid to ask if it isn't clear to you.

Allow around 45 minutes for this test. Take a short break if necessary.

In this test you will need to look at a picture or read something first. Then read each question and colour in the circle with the correct answer.

Look at the movie poster and answer question 1.

Look at the drawing and answer questions 2 to 3.

From *Art Today*, CD1/0036/LIF050.JPG

From *Art Today*, CD1/0051/QRT170.JPG

1. What is this poster about?

 ○ It is a fairy tale about a man and little people.

 ○ It is a story about something that really happened.

 ○ It is a true story about a man and little people.

 ○ It is all about little people that sing and dance.

2. What is happening in this drawing?

 ○ The rabbit is doing arithmetic.

 ○ The rabbit is working in an office.

 ○ The rabbit is checking sums.

3. Which statement is true?

 ○ This is a real rabbit.

 ○ This is a really bright rabbit.

 ○ The rabbit is making silly mistakes with the calculations.

 ○ The rabbit in this drawing cannot be real.

Read *Doctor Foster* and answer questions 4 to 5.

Doctor Foster

Doctor Foster went
to Gloucester
In a shower of rain;
He stepped in a puddle,
Right up to his middle,
And never went there again.

4. What happened to Doctor Foster?
   - ○ He forgot his umbrella.
   - ○ He tripped in a puddle of water.
   - ○ He was caught in the rain.
   - ○ He stepped in a puddle of water.

5. Which word rhymes with *Foster*?
   - ○ Gloucester
   - ○ middle
   - ○ rain
   - ○ again
   - ○ puddle

Read the story and answer questions 6 to 13.

'Do you want to come to a barbecue on Sunday, Jason? It's a Macedonian picnic.'

Our grade was getting changed for T-ball. I waited for Jason to say no.

My Mum said I had to ask him. And when Mum's made up her mind, you don't argue.

'Jason asked you to his birthday party,' she said. 'You must ask him to Saint Naum Ohridski's Monastery picnic.'

What Mum doesn't know, is that Jason asked the whole class to his party. She was just so pleased that I was invited.

Mum doesn't understand Jason was born here. He plays Aussie Rules, not soccer. He eats hamburgers, not savoury pastries like maznik or zelnik. When we had to fill in the form for Mr Burness about religious instruction classes, Jason left it blank. Jason goes to discos, not Macedonian dancing classes.

I'm the expert on dancing classes. I'm the only Macedonian kid who's had fifty-six lessons and still can't dance.

Anyway, the dancing wasn't the only reason I didn't want to ask Jason. He's popular — and I'm just a new 'Maco' kid.

Jason looked up from tying his runners. 'What time do I have to be at your place?' he asked.

That's when I nearly fell over the bat that I'm always dropping. (Dad says that instead of Pece, my name should be Clumsy.)

'About 9 o'clock,' I stuttered. 'We'll be back about 5 o'clock. Is that okay?'

'Fine. See you then, Pete.'

From *The Day My Friend Learned to Dance* by Hazel Edwards, HBJ, 1990

6. When is the barbecue?
   - ○ The barbecue is on Tuesday.
   - ○ The barbecue is after school.
   - ○ The barbecue is on Sunday.

7. Did Pece expect Jason to come to the picnic?
   - ○ Yes   ○   No

8. Why did Pece's mother tell him to ask Jason?

○ Jason asked Pece to his birthday party.

○ You don't argue with Pece's mother.

○ Jason is Pece's friend.

9. What do we learn about Jason? (Colour in more than one circle if necessary.)

○ He eats hamburgers.

○ He goes to discos.

○ He is a 'Maco' kid.

○ He is new.

○ He is popular.

○ He is religious.

○ He learns dancing.

○ He likes savoury pastries.

○ He plays Aussie Rules.

○ He plays soccer.

10. What are we told about Pece? (Colour in more than one circle if necessary.)

○ He eats hamburgers.

○ He goes to discos.

○ He is a 'Maco' kid.

○ He is new.

○ He is popular.

○ He is religious.

○ He learns dancing.

○ He likes savoury pastries.

○ He plays Aussie Rules.

○ He plays soccer.

11. Will Jason come to the barbecue?

○ Yes   ○   No

12. Was Pece surprised?

○ Yes   ○   No

13. What name does Jason call Pece?

○ Pete

○ Clumsy

○ Maco

It would be a good idea to check your answers to questions 1 to 13 before moving on to the other questions.

Read the short fable and answer questions 14 to 19.

Once upon a time a cheeky dog ran off with a bone from a butcher's shop. The greedy dog ran away as fast as it could and no one could catch it.

The dog kept on running and running until at last it came to a river bank. It stopped for a moment but as the dog looked down into the water, it saw another dog with a large bone in its mouth.

The greedy dog thought 'Why, that dog has a bone that's as big as mine, so I shall jump on that dog and take its bone for myself. Then I can have two bones.' But the silly dog did not realise that it was only seeing itself in the water.

The dog leapt in and there was a large splash of water but there was no other dog to be seen. As the greedy dog jumped in to grab the other bone, the bone that it had stolen dropped from its mouth. It sank down into the deep dark water.

Like all people who are greedy, there is nothing for them in the end. They end up with less.

14. What was in the river?

○ another dog

○ nothing

○ a reflection of the dog

15. What did the dog try to do?

○ It tried to fight the other dog.

○ It jumped into the river.

○ It tried to get another bone.

16. What is the best way to describe this dog?

○ naughty

○ greedy

○ angry

17. What happened to the dog?

○ The dog found another dog.

○ The dog tricked itself.

○ The dog kept the bone.

18. What did the dog lose?

○ The dog lost its temper.

○ The dog lost the fight.

○ The dog lost the bone.

19. What does this fable teach us?

○ It teaches us not to steal.

○ It teaches us that greedy people can lose everything.

○ It teaches us that greedy people are easy to fool.

Read the poem and answer questions 20 to 24.

The big waves are breaking

And the blue water's fine

The whole family's happy

Oh, what a great time.

There's nothing so good

As my Christmas holidays

Just fishing and swimming

And lazy old ways.

My Dad is delighted

At having a rest

No work for two weeks

He feels like he's blessed.

And Mum is so pleased

That her everyday chores

Are far from her mind

By these blue ocean shores.

Anon

20. Who is writing this poem?

○ Mum

○ Dad

○ child

21. Where is the family?

○ The family is on vacation near the sea.

○ The family is together for Christmas.

○ The family is on vacation at home.

22. Why is the mother happy?

○ The mother is happy because she can go fishing and swimming.

○ The mother is happy because the surf is fine.

○ The mother is happy because she is free from her everyday jobs.

23. Why is the father happy?
Write your answer on the lines.

_____

_____

_____

_____

24. What would be a good name for this poem?

○ Christmas Vacation

○ A Long Weekend

○ Getting Far Far Away

○ Sailing Away

Read the passage and answer questions 25 to 27.

People from all over the world flock to New York City for fame and fortune.

Think big buildings like the Empire State Building and the Rockefeller Centre. Think rap music, hip-hop, jazz, cool art, yellow taxis, graffiti on the trains and strange people in the street. Think baseball teams like the New York Yankees. New York City would have to be the MOST amazing place in the whole UNIVERSE! It's fast, big and exciting.

From *SWAT: New York City* by Lisa Thompson, Blake Education, 2000

25. Why do people *all over the world flock to New York City*?

○ to see the New York Yankees

○ to listen to rap, hip-hop and jazz music

○ to ride a yellow taxi

○ for fame and fortune

26. How does the author describe New York?

○ New York is strange and cool.

○ New York is full of rich people.

○ New York has lots of musicians and baseball players.

○ New York is fast, big and exciting.

27. Which word is different?

○ fame

○ fortune

○ fast

It would be a good idea to check your answers to questions 14 to 27 before moving on to the other questions.

Read the passage and answer questions 28 to 33.

I am a woman who stands clutching a flaming torch. I live alone on an island and am monstrously tall. I was a gift from France and arrived in the United States in 214 different crates in 1884. For many New Americans arriving by ship, I was their first glimpse of their new country. The seven points on my crown radiate to the seven continents and the seven seas.

From *SWAT: New York City* by Lisa Thompson, Blake Education, 2000

28. What would be a good title for this passage?

○ The Tall Woman

○ A Gift from France

○ A New Country

○ The Flaming Torch

29. Which of the following does NOT mean the same as a *gift*?

○ something presented to you

○ something you receive

○ something you buy

○ something offered free

30. Where did this gift come from?

○ United States

○ France

○ New America

○ the seven seas

31. Which option means the same as *clutch*?

○ release

○ unleash

○ hold tightly

○ set free

32. Which word means the same as *glimpse*?

○ idea

○ peek

○ house

○ globe

33. How many different crates did the gift come in?

○ 1884

○ 214

○ 7

○ 52

Read *Spiders* and answer questions 34 to 39.

Spiders

There are many species of spiders in Australia and Australian spiders are among the most lethal in the world. Years ago, the treatment for spider bites included cutting through the bite and sucking out the venom, or poison. Now, however, doctors have shown that putting pressure on the bitten area will stop the spread of the venom throughout the body until the victim can get to a hospital, where a doctor can help.

The funnel-web has a large body of about 3 cm long, and together with its legs can cover an adult hand. The funnel-web is very aggressive and has been responsible for several deaths in Australia.

The signs of a funnel-web spider bite are:

• pain
• heavy sweating
• stomach pain
• twitching of muscles
• trouble breathing.

To give first aid for funnel-web spider bites, follow this procedure:

1. Put pressure on the bitten area, bandage up the area tightly and don't move the body at all.
2. Keep the victim calm and at rest.
3. Call an ambulance or doctor immediately.

34. Which of the following are signs of a funnel-web spider bite?

○ rash, weakness, vomiting
○ trouble breathing, heavy sweating, stomach pain
○ bleeding, itching, sweating
○ back pain, headache, cramps

35. What should you do if a funnel-web spider bites you? Colour in one circle.

○ put an ice-pack on the bitten area
○ cut through the bite and suck out the venom
○ wash the bite, then cover it with a bandaid
○ bandage up the area tightly and don't move the victim at all

36. When should the victim seek medical help?

○ suddenly
○ slowly
○ never
○ immediately

37. Verbs are doing words. Which of these words from the passage are BOTH verbs? Colour in one circle.

○ cutting, doctor
○ stop, help
○ venom, victim
○ have, most

38. Which statement is true? Colour in one circle.

○ Funnel-web spiders are as long as an adult's finger.

○ Australian spiders are not lethal.

○ The way to treat a bite is to cut it and suck out the venom.

○ The victim should try to move their legs once bitten.

○ The funnel-web spider measures 3 cm long.

○ Putting pressure on the bite will stop the venom spreading.

39. Which word means the same as *aggressive*?

○ helpless

○ delicate

○ fragile

○ violent

END OF TEST

Well done! You have completed the second Reading Test. This test had different types of questions. They are like comprehension passages. You had to look at something or read something and then make a judgement.

How did you find these questions? We hope that you found them interesting. Revise anything that was too hard for you. There are further questions in the next Reading Test. The next test contains some different questions. Now take a long break before doing any more tests.

Use the diagnostic chart on page 73 to see which level of ability you reached. This is only an estimate. Don't be surprised if you answered some difficult questions correctly or even missed some easier questions.

Please note that multiple interpretations are possible for the levels of difficulty of these tasks. Also, some questions involve skills from different levels. This is only an initial guide to the approximate level of the reading skill assessed.

Instructions

As you check the answer for each question, mark it as correct (✓) or incorrect (✗). Mark any questions that you omitted or left out as incorrect (✗) for the moment.

Then look at how many you answered correctly in each level. You will be able to see what level you are at by finding the point where you started having consistent difficulty with questions at a certain level. For example, if you answer most questions correctly up to the Intermediate level and then get most questions wrong from then onwards, it is likely your ability is at the Intermediate level. You can ask your parents or your teacher to help you do this if it isn't clear to you.

Am I able to ...

	SKILL	ESTIMATED LEVEL	✓ or ✗
1	Make some meaning from a picture?	Standard	
2	Find clearly stated information?	Standard	
3	Make some meaning from a picture?	Standard	
4	Make some meaning from short texts that have simple sentences?	Standard	
5	Make connections between words that rhyme?	Advanced	
6	Find clearly stated information?	Standard	
7	Find clearly stated information?	Standard	
8	Make connections between pieces of clearly stated information?	Standard	
9	Find clearly stated information?	Standard	
10	Make connections between pieces of clearly stated information?	Standard	
11	Find information?	Standard	
12	Find information?	Standard	
13	Find clearly stated information?	Standard	
14	Make connections between pieces of clearly stated information?	Intermediate	
15	Interpret information?	Intermediate	
16	Describe a character?	Intermediate	
17	Identify events?	Intermediate	
18	Identify events?	Intermediate	
19	Identify the main idea?	Intermediate	
20	Interpret information?	Intermediate	
21	Interpret information?	Intermediate	
22	Interpret information?	Intermediate	
23	Interpret information?	Intermediate	
24	Identify the title?	Standard	
25	Find clearly stated information?	Standard	
26	Identify the author's description?	Intermediate	
27	Separate an adjective from nouns?	Intermediate	
28	Identify the title of a text?	Advanced	
29	Identify the meaning of a word?	Intermediate	
30	Find clearly stated information?	Standard	
31	Identify the meaning of a word?	Intermediate	
32	Identify the meaning of a word?	Intermediate	
33	Find clearly stated information?	Standard	
34	Find clearly stated information?	Standard	
35	Find clearly stated information?	Standard	
36	Connect information?	Intermediate	
37	Identify verbs?	Advanced	
38	Validate a conclusion?	Advanced	
39	Identify the meaning of a word?	Intermediate	
	TOTAL		

ADAPTED FOR
ONLINE
FORMAT

This is the third Reading Test. There are 39 questions.

If you aren't sure what to do, ask your teacher or your parents to help you. Don't be afraid to ask if it isn't clear to you.

Allow around 45 minutes for this test. Take a short break if necessary.

In this test you will need to look at a picture or read something first. Then read each question and colour in the circle with the correct answer.

Read the label and answer questions 1 to 4.

LEMONADE
a product of
The Rocka-Cola Company

LEMONADE
Prepared and bottled by Rocka-Cola,
142 Soda Street, Melbourne 3000,
Australia
'Brite' contains carbonated water,
sugar, food acid (339, 443), flavours,
preservative (654)

CONSUMER INFORMATION CALL 4567 8910
© 2020 THE ROCKA-COLA COMPANY

1. In which country is Brite! prepared?

   ○ Melbourne

   ○ America

   ○ Australia

   ○ Britain

Did you colour in one of the circles?

2. What is the main purpose of this label?

   ○ The label makes you buy more Brite!

   ○ The label provides instructions for making lemonade.

   ○ The label informs customers as to what is in the bottle or can.

   ○ The label tells the story of the Rocka-Cola Company.

---

3. Which word is similar in meaning to *consumer*?

   ○ seller

   ○ supplier

   ○ provider

   ○ purchaser

4. Which preservative is found in Brite?

339	654	443	142
○	○	○	○

Look at the book cover and answer questions 5 to 6.

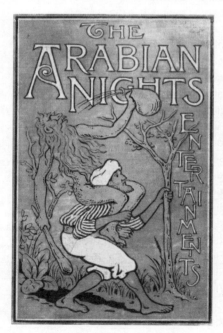

From *Art Today*, CD2/0155/END000CB.JPG

---

5. Which statement is true?

   ○ It is a children's book about the evening sky.

   ○ It is an adult book about tales of men wrestling.

   ○ It is a book of wonderful tales of the Arab world.

Did you colour in one of the circles?

6. What type of things would you find in this book?

   ○ kings, queens, knights, castles

   ○ sultans, princes, camels, oases

   ○ goblins, fairies, witches, elves

Read the text and answer questions 7 to 10.

Greenplace Primary School
invites you to attend their
125th anniversary

FETE
and ART EXHIBITION

Saturday, December 17, 2022
10 am to 4 pm

COME AND JOIN THE FUN!
· Great Stalls · Rides · Wonderful Food
· Entertainment · Children's Games
· Auctions of Sports Memorabilia
... and much more!!!

Greenplace Primary School
Cnr Turner Bay Rd & Byron St

7. What type of text is this?

   ○ a poem

   ○ a web page

   ○ an advertisement

   ○ an invitation

8. Who is inviting you to the fete?

   ○ the staff

   ○ the parents

   ○ Greenplace Primary School

   ○ the Principal at Greenplace Primary School

9. At what time will the fete be open?

   ○ 10 am to 2 pm

   ○ 10 pm to 4 am

   ○ 10 am to 4 pm

   ○ 10 am to 7 pm

10. Who might be receiving these invitations?

    ○ the school staff

    ○ family members

    ○ the school pupils

    ○ all of the above

Look at the drawing and answer questions 11 to 12.

Mine

From *Art Today*, CD2/0088/GA4058.JPG

11. What is the girl doing in the drawing?

- ○ She is following the footprints of the dog.
- ○ She is on the beach.
- ○ She is playing with her dog.
- ○ She is a scientist.

12. The drawing shows that

- ○ this dog is smarter than the girl.
- ○ this girl is smarter than the dog.
- ○ this dog can talk to the girl.

It would be a good idea to check your answers to questions 1 to 12 before moving on to the other questions.

Read the poem and answer questions 13 to 15.

With a twig in your beak
Busy building a nest
You stop for a moment
To take a brief rest.

You know what to do
And where you should go
How to work quickly
And when to be slow.

You live in a world
So free of our cares
With only the present
And Nature's affairs.

Little bird in the tree
Such a glorious sight
Your work is now done
With the coming of night.

Anon

13. What would be a good name for this poem?

- ○ A Bird
- ○ With a Twig in Your Beak
- ○ Anon
- ○ Little Bird in the Tree

14. Who is 'busy' in this poem?

- ○ the bird
- ○ the nest
- ○ the building

15. Which word in the poem means the same as *worries*?

- ○ cares   ○ affairs
- ○ moment   ○ free

Read *Muddles and Mix-ups* and answer questions 16 to 21.

Muddles and Mix-ups

You often find several children in the one school who have the same name.

There might be two Michaels or four Sarahs or three Matthews.

The first Matthew may be short and fair.

The second Matthew may be medium-sized with red hair and freckles.

The third Matthew may be tall and dark-haired.

But the name Matthew suits all three because their names have grown on them.

When you meet someone else with the same name as yours, it's natural to feel a little curious about the other person.

Say your name is Bianca and you meet another Bianca. You can't help wondering, can you, what the other Bianca is like. Is she friendly? Are you going to like her?

Names can sometimes cause confusion. Here is an example.

The three Smith sisters all have names beginning with the letter M. They are called Melinda, Marlene and Melissa.

Think how confusing it can be when the family receives a letter addressed to M Smith!

In a case like this, it's a good idea to address a letter in full, to Melinda Smith (or Marlene Smith or Melissa Smith). Then there can be no mistake.

From *Names are Fun* by Vivienne Wallington, HBJ, 1992

16. What is an example of sharing names?
- ○ when your name fits you
- ○ when there are two Michaels in a school
- ○ when your name has grown on you

17. What does the third Matthew look like?
- ○ He is short and fair.
- ○ He is medium-sized with red hair and freckles.
- ○ He is tall and dark-haired.

18. When do some people feel curious?
- ○ People feel curious when they meet someone with the same name.
- ○ People feel curious when they meet someone who is friendly.
- ○ People feel curious when they meet someone who is nice.

19. What is a muddle?
- ○ It is an example.
- ○ It is a mix-up.
- ○ It is a name.

20. When does confusion occur?
- ○ when the letter is addressed to Melinda Smith
- ○ when the letter is addressed to Marlene Smith
- ○ when the letter is addressed to M Smith
- ○ when the letter is addressed to Melissa Smith

21. Who wondered what someone else is like?
- ○ Matthew
- ○ Bianca
- ○ Melinda
- ○ Marlene

Read the instructions and answer questions 22 to 25.

Iron-On Transfer Instructions

1. Most important, ask Mum or Dad to help.
2. Do not use a pure cotton fabric—use nylon or polyester.
3. Do your ironing on a hard surface such as a magazine.
4. Place the transfer facedown on a single piece of fabric.
5. Pin the transfer into position so that it does not move.
6. Set the setting on the iron to 'COTTON'.
7. Do not scorch the fabric. Cover the area to be ironed with brown paper or tissue paper.
8. Press down hard and move the iron around smoothly.
9. Iron for about 20 seconds.

CAUTION: NOT INTENDED FOR CHILDREN UNDER 8—TO BE USED WITH ADULT HELP

22. What is the most important instruction?

- ○ Ask Mum or Dad to help.
- ○ Do not use cotton.
- ○ Iron for about 20 seconds.

23. Which fabric should be used?

- ○ polyester
- ○ silk
- ○ cotton

24. How long should it be ironed for?

- ○ 15 seconds
- ○ 20 seconds
- ○ 25 seconds

25. For what age group is this recommended?

- ○ children over 5 years with adult help
- ○ children over 6 years with adult help
- ○ children over 7 years with adult help
- ○ children over 8 years with adult help

It would be a good idea to check your answers to questions 13 to 25 before moving on to the other questions.

Read *Bogies* and answer questions 26 to 31.

Bogies

Once upon a time, when children were naughty, parents said: 'A bogy will get you!'

What is a bogy?

A bogy is a mischievous or frightening or dangerous spirit. Bogy is a very old word and it comes from the British Isles, from a time when people believed in the world of fairies, goblins and ghosts.

Adults used to frighten children by telling them about many different kinds of bogies. Some lived in water, others waited in fruit trees, and many hid in dark places, indoors and out.

Adults were afraid of bogies too, especially the kind that lurked on the roads on dark nights, lying in wait for the traveller.

Why did adults scare children with bogy stories?

There were three main reasons:

1. To protect crops from children's stealing fingers.
2. To keep children away from dangerous places.
3. To make children behave.

From *A Bogy Will Get You* by Edel Wignell, HBJ, 1992

26. Which statement is true?

- ○ A bogy is not a real thing.
- ○ A bogy is a real thing.

27. What are we told about bogies?

- ○ Bogies were frightened of children.
- ○ Bogies were frightened of adults.
- ○ Adults were afraid of bogies.

28. Where did the word *bogy* come from?

- ○ It came from the British Isles.
- ○ It came from children.
- ○ It came from Australia.

29. What type of bogies frightened adults?

- ○ the bogies that lived in water
- ○ the bogies that were on roads on dark nights
- ○ the bogies that lived in fruit trees

30. Which of the three reasons given for adults scaring the children with bogies is related to the opening sentence?

- ○ to protect crops
- ○ to keep children away from danger
- ○ to make children behave

31. Which word in the fifth paragraph means the same as *waited*?

- ○ believed
- ○ lurked
- ○ hid
- ○ lying

Read *Australian-made* and answer questions 32 to 39.

Australian-made

Each country has its own version of slang, newcomers to our land may never have heard our kind of slang, and certainly would not understand its meaning. What must they think when they hear talk of a smoko (rest break) or hard yakka (work) or a crawler (someone looking for praise) or a blue (fight) or snags on the barbie (barbecued sausages)? They may want to reach for a dictionary to help them translate foreign speech!

Australians are famous for their use of colourful expressions and sayings. For two hundred years we have been using old slang words, inventing new ones and perhaps forgetting some that may go in and out of fashion as times and sayings change. In fact, Aussies invent words to describe everyday events in their lives. This can be confusing for non-Australians. Not only are the words new to them, but one word can have lots of different meanings. For example, if a car is hot, it's probably stolen; if a person is wearing hot clothes, they look trendy; if someone is a hot guitarist, it means they are skillful; and a hotshot in tennis is a person with lots of potential.

From *Dinky-Di* by Shane Power, HBJ, 1992

32. What is slang?

- ○ Slang is the special sayings that a certain group of people use.
- ○ Slang is a foreign language.
- ○ Slang is the correct English that we use in Australia.
- ○ Slang is used only in Australia.

33. After some work in the garden, the workers have a rest break.

Change this sentence into slang.

Write your answer in the space provided.

_____

_____

_____

_____

34. Why is the article called *Australian-made*?

    ○ *Australian-made* is about the colourful expressions used in every country.

    ○ *Australian-made* is about the problems newcomers have with the language in Australia.

    ○ *Australian-made* is about the colourful language that has been developed in this country.

    ○ *Australian-made* is about the products made in Australia.

35. For what are Australians famous?

    ○ Australians are famous for their use of colourful language.

    ○ Australians are famous for snags on the barbie.

    ○ Australians are famous for their smokos and cuppas.

36. For about how long have Australians been using old slang words?

    ○ for about 100 years

    ○ for about 200 years

    ○ for about 300 years

37. What is an example of a slang word that can have more than one meaning?

    ○ smoko

    ○ cuppa

    ○ hot

    ○ crawler

38. What is the role of the first sentence in both paragraphs?

    ○ The first sentence tells the reader what each paragraph is about.

    ○ The first sentence tells the reader a true story.

    ○ The first sentence tells the reader what is important.

39. What would create confusion for a newcomer?

    ○ Newcomers may never have heard our slang.

    ○ reaching for a dictionary to help them translate slang

    ○ the words that describe everyday life

END OF TEST

Well done! You have completed the third Reading Test. This test also had some different types of questions. Some involved pictures and some were like comprehension passages.

We hope that these tasks were interesting for you. How did you find these questions? Revise anything that was hard for you. There are further questions in the final Reading Test.

Use the diagnostic chart on page 81 to see which level of ability you reached. This is only an estimate. Don't be surprised if you answered some difficult questions correctly or even missed some easier questions.

Please note that multiple interpretations are possible for the levels of difficulty of these tasks. Also, some questions involve skills from different levels. This is only an initial guide to the approximate level of the reading skill assessed. No claim is made that this will be identical to the scores a student will receive in the actual tests, as the assessors will use a complex scoring system to estimate a student's level of ability.

Instructions

As you check the answer for each question, mark it as correct (✓) or incorrect (✗). Mark any questions that you omitted or left out as incorrect (✗) for the moment.

Then look at how many you answered correctly in each level. You will be able to see what level you are at by finding the point where you started having consistent difficulty with questions at a certain level. For example, if you answer most questions correctly up to the Intermediate level and then get most questions wrong from then onwards, it is likely your ability is at the Intermediate level. You can ask your parents or your teacher to help you do this if it isn't clear to you.

Am I able to ...

	SKILL	ESTIMATED LEVEL	✓ or ✗
1	Find clearly stated information?	Standard	
2	Identify the purpose?	Intermediate	
3	Identify the meaning of a word?	Intermediate	
4	Find clearly stated information?	Standard	
5	Make meaning from a text which has visual support?	Standard	
6	Make simple inferences?	Intermediate	
7	Identify a style of writing?	Intermediate	
8	Make meaning from a simple advertisement?	Standard	
9	Find clearly stated information?	Standard	
10	Draw conclusions?	Intermediate	
11	Infer from the action in a drawing?	Advanced	
12	Draw an inference from a cartoon?	Advanced	
13	Identify the title of a text?	Intermediate	
14	Find clearly stated information?	Standard	
15	Find an equivalent word?	Advanced	
16	Compare and connect information?	Intermediate	
17	Identify details?	Standard	
18	Infer a personal state of feeling?	Advanced	
19	Identify the meaning of a word?	Intermediate	
20	Interpret information?	Intermediate	
21	Locate a person who matches a description?	Intermediate	
22	Identify the priority of an idea?	Intermediate	
23	Make connections between pieces of clearly stated information?	Standard	
24	Identify clearly stated information?	Standard	
25	Identify the limitations of the instructions?	Intermediate	
26	Indicate the truth of an idea?	Intermediate	
27	Identify a fact from the text?	Intermediate	
28	Identify a fact from the text?	Intermediate	
29	Connect information?	Intermediate	
30	Relate the introduction to the conclusion?	Advanced	
31	Explain a word's meaning?	Advanced	
32	Infer the meaning of a word?	Advanced	
33	Translate a sentence into slang?	Intermediate	
34	Identify the relevance of a title?	Advanced	
35	Locate information?	Intermediate	
36	Locate information?	Standard	
37	Identify a word with multiple meaning?	Advanced	
38	Recognise the purpose of the opening sentence of a paragraph?	Advanced	
39	Explain a phenomenon?	Intermediate	
	TOTAL		

This is the final Reading Test. There are 39 questions.

If you aren't sure what to do, ask your teacher or your parents to help you. Don't be afraid to ask if it isn't clear to you.

Allow around 45 minutes for this test. Take a short rest break if necessary.

In this part you will need to look at a picture or read something first. Then read each question and colour in the circle with the correct answer.

Look at *Lands & Peoples* and answer question 1.

From *Art Today*, CD4/0259/CAW000C.JPG

1. What does the name of the book *Lands & Peoples* tell you?

   ○ It's about other countries and their people.

   ○ It's about the land and the people who work on it.

   ○ It's about how people landed in different countries.

   ○ It's about England.

Did you colour in one of the circles?

Look at the cartoon and answer questions 2 to 3.

From *Art Today*, CD1/0057/NYW224B–C.JPG

2. What is happening in the first part of this cartoon?

   ○ The man is taking two tyres from someone else's car.

   ○ The man is bringing two tyres to his own car.

   ○ The man is bringing two tyres to someone else's car.

   ○ The man has lost four tyres from his car.

3. Which statement is true about the man in the second picture?

   ○ He looks suspicious.

   ○ He looks astonished.

   ○ He looks happy.

   ○ He looks satisfied.

Read *My Pants Have Sprung a Huge Hole* and answer questions 4 to 9.

My Pants Have Sprung a Huge Hole

A week before Christmas, on a wintry night,

Snow lay around like a blanket of white.

The air was bitter, colder than ice

And no one went out without thinking twice.

Then all of a sudden a voice thundered out

Piercing the silence that lay all about.

It shouted so loud, so sharp and so clear,

That voice was meant
   for the whole world to hear.

Booming from somewhere
   up in the North Pole,

The voice said: 'My pants
   have sprung a huge hole!

Look at the back of me! See the big tear!

You could park a gigantic battleship there!

It's against the law – a crime do you hear?

For a chap like me to expose his rear!

How can I possibly go, "Ho, ho ho!"

With my underpants all out on show?'

Then Santa himself appeared at the door,

Hands covering the rip, which tore a
   bit more.

With forehead so wrinkled and face so cross,

He spluttered, 'Is this how you treat
   your boss?

One of you elves must be playing a joke—

A mighty mean thing to do to a bloke!'

From Ho, Ho, Ho! by Jan Weeks, HBJ, 1992

4. Who wrote this poem?
   ○ Santa Claus
   ○ The Elves
   ○ Jan Weeks
   ○ My Pants Have Sprung a Huge Hole

5. What happened in this poem?
   ○ There was a hole in Santa's pants.
   ○ There was a hole in the Elves' pants.
   ○ There was a hole in Santa's jacket.

6. When did all this happen?
   ○ It happened after Christmas.
   ○ It happened at Christmas.
   ○ It happened a week before Christmas.

7. What things tell you for sure that it was cold? (Colour in as many circles as necessary.)
   ○ It was a week before Christmas.
   ○ It was against the law.
   ○ It was at the North Pole.
   ○ It was night.
   ○ It was silent.
   ○ The air was cold.
   ○ There was a gigantic battleship there.
   ○ There was snow.

8. How do we know Santa was angry?
   ○ He was angry because he was loud and cross.
   ○ He was angry because he appeared at the door.
   ○ He was angry because he said that it was mean to do this to him.

9. What does the word *bloke* mean?

○ a man

○ a mate

○ something torn

○ a mean thing

Did you colour in one of the circles?

Read *How to Be a Magician* and answer questions 10 to 15.

How to Be A Magician

You can be a magician!

The secret of being a successful magician is learning how to do tricks properly. There are three main ingredients in this recipe for success: preparation, practice and patter.

Preparation

Preparation means having all your props and clothing ready in advance.

Props are the particular items you need to perform each trick.

For clothing you need a jacket or a long-sleeved shirt with pockets and buttons. Trousers should have pockets where you can hide things. A belt is a good idea too, as you can attach all kinds of things to it.

You will need a table, and a cloth which is large enough to hang down to the floor on three sides. Use drawing-pins or tape to hold the cloth in place. The side facing you should be open, so that you can store all your props under the table where the audience cannot see them.

From *How to be a Magician* by Rachael Collinson, HBJ, 1992

10. What would be another good name for this passage?

○ Ten Terrific Tricks

○ How to Trick Your Family and Friends

○ How to Do Magic Tricks

11. What is this passage about?

○ preparation

○ practice

○ patter

12. How many ingredients are listed?

1	2	3	4
○	○	○	○

13. What does *preparation* mean?

○ It means being a successful magician.

○ It means having everything ready.

○ It means learning how to do tricks properly.

14. What is *patter*?

○ talking

○ props

○ practice

15. What clothing does a magician need?
(Colour in more than one circle if necessary.)

- ○ belt
- ○ drawing pins
- ○ jacket
- ○ magic wand
- ○ pockets where you can hide things
- ○ props
- ○ shirt with long sleeves, pockets and buttons
- ○ shirt with short sleeves, pockets and buttons
- ○ table cloth
- ○ tape
- ○ trousers

It would be a good idea to check your answers to questions 1 to 15 before moving on to the other questions.

Read *Healthy Food Builds Healthy Bodies* and answer questions 16 to 20.

Healthy Food Builds Healthy Bodies

To eat a healthy, balanced diet we should choose a variety of the following foods each day. These provide plenty of fibre and are low in sugar, salt and fat.

- Fresh fruit
- Fresh vegetables
- Sprouts, nuts and seeds
- Soya beans and lentils
- Cereals and wholegrain products including bread, rice and pasta
- Dairy products like milk, cheese and yoghurt
- Eggs (preferably free-range)
- Cold-pressed oils, spreadable fats like unsalted butter

Only eat meat, fish and poultry occasionally.

Chewing food properly before you swallow it is very important. Even nutritious food can be bad for you if you eat it too quickly or eat too much of it. Always make time to sit down and relax when you eat your food. Eating good food can be lots of fun, especially if you take time to prepare and enjoy your meals.

From *Fun with Food* by Eleanor Parker, HBJ, 1992

16. Why is healthy food important?

- ○ Healthy food makes you stronger.
- ○ Healthy food gives you balance.
- ○ Healthy food gives you a diet.

17. Which foods are said to be low in sugar, salt or fat?

- ○ meat
- ○ poultry
- ○ salted butter
- ○ fresh fruit

18. What foods are included with cereals?

- ○ fresh fruit
- ○ meat, fish and poultry
- ○ milk, cheese and yoghurt
- ○ bread, rice and pasta

19. What does *occasionally* mean?

- ○ once every now and then
- ○ once every day
- ○ at every meal
- ○ once a year

20. Choose the best meaning for the word *digesting*.

○ using

○ eating

○ building

○ balancing

Read *Indonesia* and answer questions 21 to 26.

INDONESIA

Indonesia is one of Australia's closest neighbours. This is a map of Indonesia. It is made up of over 13 000 small islands. People live on about 6000 of these islands.

Indonesia is between the Indian and Pacific Oceans. It is near the equator and has a hot climate. Rice and fish are two of the main products. The region is mostly coastal and some of the larger islands have mountains. There are 60 active volcanos in Indonesia.

Indonesia is a large nation of some 200 million people and is the fifth largest country in the world. Most of the people are of a Muslim background, with some Christians, Buddhists and Hindus. They speak mainly Bahasa Indonesia. For many years Indonesia was a Dutch colony and it gained independence just after World War II. Indonesia has been a poor country but this is starting to change.

It has a rich tradition and culture. Many Australians like to visit Bali, which is a favourite cultural and holiday centre.

21. How many islands are there in Indonesia?

○ 13 000

○ 60

○ 6000

○ 200 million

22. On how many islands do people live?

○ 13 000

○ 60

○ 6000

○ 200 million

23. What are two of Indonesia's products?

○ rice, fish

○ coasts, mountains

24. How large is Indonesia?

○ It is the fifth largest country in the world.

○ It is mainly a Muslim country.

○ People live on about 6000 islands.

25. Between which two oceans is Indonesia?

○ Indonesia is between Borneo and Sumatra.

○ Indonesia is between Jakarta and Sumatra.

○ Indonesia is between Australia and Borneo.

○ Indonesia is between the Indian and Pacific Oceans.

26. Which part of Indonesia do Australians visit frequently?

○ Borneo

○ Bali

○ Sumatra

○ Jakarta

It would be a good idea to check your answers to questions 16 to 26 before moving on to the other questions.

Read the passage and answer questions 27 to 34.

Joanne's father owned a milk bar and sandwich shop in Bondi, a Sydney beachside suburb. Joanne and her Dad lived at the back of the shop in four tiny, cluttered and untidy rooms. Joanne's mum died  when she was three. Joanne had wonderful memories of her mum. Memories of a soft voice, cuddles, bed-time stories and having her hair brushed.

Joanne loved her father and loved their home. She had always been her Dad's girl, although she had her mother's smile. Dad read her stories and gave her cuddles too, but it was difficult for him to make time for an 8 year old. He opened the shop at 8 o'clock in the morning and didn't finish until 9 o'clock at night. Then there was the cooking and the housework to be done, and Joanne's school clothes to be washed and ironed every night.

Just before storytime, Joanne would go into the shop and share a milkshake with her father. Dad's milkshakes were a real treat: double milk, malt, two scoops of ice cream, and chocolate flavouring.

Often Dad's friend Graham Willis would be there too. Graham, a police sergeant, would call in for a chat on his way to or from work.

From *Joanne* by Paul Williams, HBJ, 1992

27. What did Joanne's father own?

○ He owned a grocery and sandwich shop.

○ He owned a seafood shop in Bondi.

○ He owned four rooms.

○ He owned a milk bar and sandwich shop.

28. Where did Joanne live?

○ Joanne lived with her parents.

○ Joanne lived at the back of Bondi.

○ Joanne lived at the back of the shop.

29. How old was Joanne when her mother died?

○ 3 years old

○ 5 years old

○ 8 years old

30. Who read bedtime stories to Joanne?

○ Her father's friend read bedtime stories to Joanne.

○ Joanne read bedtime stories to herself.

○ Joanne's father read bedtime stories to Joanne.

31. When did Joanne's father finish work?

○ He finished at 9 o'clock.

○ He finished at 8 o'clock.

○ He finished just before storytime.

32. What was in the milkshakes her father made?

○ milk scoops, ice cream and chocolate flavouring

○ milk, malt, ice cream and chocolate flavouring

○ milk, malt, cream and chocolate

33. Why was Graham Willis there?

○ He was a police sergeant.

○ He read her stories.

○ He called in for a chat.

34. Why was it difficult for Joanne's father to make time for her?

○ She went to school during the day.

○ Her mother passed away when she was three.

○ He made special milkshakes for her before storytime.

○ He worked from 8 am in the morning until 9 pm at night.

Did you colour in one of the circles?

Read the passage and answer questions 35 to 38.

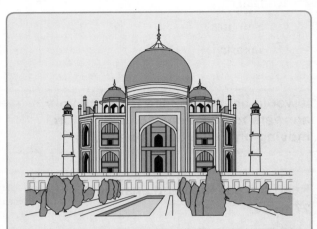

This time Amber made a perfect landing right in front of the Taj Mahal. Jeremy landed a few seconds later. Habbibi didn't even question his new form of transport. All he said was, 'This is very handy. One day I hope to be able to travel like this on my own.'

India has many beautiful buildings, but none are more famous than the Taj Mahal. The white marble building glistened in the sun.

'It's so beautiful!' gasped Amber.

Habbibi proudly explained the story behind it. 'It was built many centuries ago by an emperor named Shah Jahan. He was very rich and he loved his wife deeply. When she died he was heart-broken so he built this in her memory. It took 20 000 workers 21 years to build.'

From SWAT: Incredible India by Lisa Thompson, Blake Education, 2000

35. What would be a good title for this passage?

- ○ Amber, Jeremy and Habbibi on their Magical Journey.
- ○ An Emperor named Shah Jahan.
- ○ The Taj Mahal.
- ○ A Day in India.

36. Who built the Taj Mahal?

- ○ Habibi
- ○ The Emperor Taj
- ○ Shah Jahan
- ○ Amber

37. How many years did it take to build?

- ○ 20 000
- ○ 176
- ○ 12
- ○ 21

38. Amber said, 'It's so beautiful!' This is

- ○ a statement.
- ○ a question.
- ○ an exclamation.
- ○ a comment.

Read The Story of Apples and answer question 39.

39. Seeds and fruit grow from flowers. Each flower must be pollinated before it can make fruit and seeds. Number the following sentences in order from 1 to 7 so the text makes sense.

The Story of Apples

[ ] When the apples are ripe they are picked and then packed into cartons.

[ ] The petals drop off the flower and the apple grows.

[ ] Seeds are planted in the ground and watered regularly.

[ ] Flowers begin as tight buds. These are the buds of apple tree flowers.

[ ] The fruit is taken to the market and sold.

[ ] The apple blossoms open. Bees or other insects carry pollen from one flower to another. This is called pollination

[ ] As the apple tree begins to grow, the plants are sprayed to keep the pests away.

Write your answers in the boxes.

END OF TEST

We hope that these tasks were interesting for you. There are no further Reading Tests. Now take a long break before you do any more tests.

Question 39 is not an easy question. You did well if you were able to put the sentences in the correct order. Revise anything that was hard for you.

Use the diagnostic chart on page 90 to see which level of ability you reached. This is only an estimate. Don't be surprised if you answered some difficult questions correctly or even missed some easier questions. Get some help if you don't understand something.

Please note that multiple interpretations are possible for the levels of difficulty of these tasks. Also, some questions involve skills from different levels. This is only an initial guide to the approximate level of the reading skill assessed. No claim is made that this will be identical to the scores a student will receive in the actual tests, as the assessors will use a complex scoring system to estimate a student's level of ability.

Instructions

As you check the answer for each question, mark it as correct (✓) or incorrect (✗). Mark any questions that you omitted or left out as incorrect (✗) for the moment.

Then look at how many you answered correctly in each level. You will be able to see what level you are at by finding the point where you started having consistent difficulty with questions at a certain level. For example, if you answer most questions correctly up to the Intermediate level and then get most questions wrong from then onwards, it is likely your ability is at the Intermediate level. You can ask your parents or your teacher to help you do this if it isn't clear to you.

Am I able to ...

	SKILL	ESTIMATED LEVEL	✓ or ✗
1	Identify purpose from a title?	Intermediate	
2	Make meaning from pictures?	Standard	
3	Infer emotion from a picture?	Advanced	
4	Identify the author?	Intermediate	
5	Make meaning from a short text?	Intermediate	
6	Find clearly stated information?	Standard	
7	Make meaning from a short text?	Standard	
8	Infer an emotion from a short text?	Standard	
9	Identify the meaning of words?	Intermediate	
10	Identify an alternative title?	Intermediate	
11	Draw an inference?	Advanced	
12	Find clearly stated information?	Standard	
13	Make meaning of a concept?	Intermediate	
14	Define a word?	Advanced	
15	Find clearly stated information?	Standard	
16	Identify a common idea from the title?	Intermediate	
17	Interpret an idea in a simple text?	Intermediate	
18	Find clearly stated information?	Standard	
19	Identify the meaning of a word?	Intermediate	
20	Choose the best meaning for a word?	Intermediate	
21	Find clearly stated information?	Standard	
22	Find clearly stated information?	Standard	
23	Find clearly stated information?	Standard	
24	Find clearly stated information?	Standard	
25	Identify a fact from the text and from a diagram?	Standard	
26	Identify a fact from the text?	Standard	
27	Find clearly stated information?	Standard	
28	Find clearly stated information?	Standard	
29	Find clearly stated information?	Standard	
30	Identify a fact from the text?	Standard	
31	Identify a fact from the text?	Standard	
32	Identify a fact from the text?	Standard	
33	Infer motivation?	Advanced	
34	Explain a fact?	Intermediate	
35	Find a title?	Advanced	
36	Locate information?	Standard	
37	Identify a fact from the text?	Standard	
38	Recognise an exclamation?	Advanced	
39	Sequence events?	Advanced	
	TOTAL		

This is the first Conventions of Language Test. There are 50 questions.

If you aren't sure what to do, ask your teacher or your parents to help you.

Don't be afraid to ask if it isn't clear to you.

Allow around 45 minutes for this test. Take a short break if necessary.

Each sentence has one word or punctuation mark that is incorrect. The mistake in the sentence is underlined. Colour in the circle with the correct answer.

Did you colour in one of the circles?

1. The big area in the middle of Australia <u>are</u> called the outback.

   is   am   be
   ◯   ◯   ◯

2. The girl asked, 'Do people live there<u>_</u>'.

   ,   !   ?
   ◯   ◯   ◯

3. He said, <u>_</u>It's a hot and dry place.'

   '   "   ,
   ◯   ◯   ◯

4. <u>Jacks</u> Dad smiled.

   Jacks'   Jac's   Jack's
   ◯   ◯   ◯

5. <u>Ive</u> never been there.

   I've   Ive'   I'v
   ◯   ◯   ◯

6. You can <u>sees</u> many kangaroos and wallabies.

   saw   seen   see
   ◯   ◯   ◯

7. There <u>am</u> many cattle in the outback.

   is   are   was
   ◯   ◯   ◯

Read the text *Dragons*. The mistakes are underlined. Colour in the circle with the word you you think is correct. There isn't a mistake in every question but you must still colour in one circle for each answer.

Dragons

8. Where did dragons <u>come</u> from?

   comes ○   came ○   come ○

9. Some say that they were real creatures which <u>live</u> many years ago.

   live ○   lives ○   lived ○

10. In one story the first dragon <u>tame</u> the floods by digging big ditches.

    tames ○   tamer ○   tamed ○

    In another story, the dragon grew inside a

11. large egg at the bottom of the sea. <u>when</u> it

    when ○   When ○

12. floated to the surface, <u>its</u> bright colours made someone pick it up.

    its ○   it's ○   its' ○

13. They took it to the beach and <u>their</u> it lay for many years.

    Their ○   there ○   There ○

    When the egg hatched the baby dragon grew very large. It caused a great storm,

14. and flew up into <u>heaven</u>

    heaven. ○   heaven! ○   heaven? ○

Adapted from *Dragons of China* by Ida Chionh, HBJ, 1992

Read the text *Vegetables*. There are three answers underlined. Only one is correct. Choose the correct word.

Vegetables

15. Vegetables are an important food **for / in / to** people around the world.

   ○ for   ○ in   ○ to

16. Pumpkins and tomatoes are vegetables that contain seeds. Scientists call them fruit because **they is / them are / they are** part of the plant that carries the seed.

   ○ they is   ○ them are   ○ they are

17. Some vegetables grow **under the ground, / under the ground. / under the ground?**

   ○ under the ground,   ○ under the ground.   ○ under the ground?

From *Go Facts – Plants as Food*, Blake Education, 2006

Choose the circle with the right answer.

18. Which word in this sentence is a noun?

   The tired boy is sleeping and he is snoring loudly.

   ○ The
   ○ tired
   ○ boy
   ○ sleeping

19. Which word in this sentence is used as an adjective?

   The girl wears a white shirt when she plays sport.

   ○ girl
   ○ white
   ○ shirt
   ○ plays

> Did you colour in one of the circles?

20. Which words can replace the pronoun *they* in this sentence?

   Jenny said that the school will have a big tent when they go camping tomorrow.

   ○ the school
   ○ the student
   ○ the girls
   ○ Jenny and me

21. *I've* is short for *I have*. What does *I'd* stand for?

   ○ I would   ○ I said   ○ I did

22. Why does the word *Tokyo* need a capital letter?

   ○ It is a large city.

   ○ It looks good.

   ○ It is a proper noun.

   ○ Many people live in Tokyo.

23. Drago came from Serbia and he is happy to be in Australia.

In this sentence the word *came* is

   ○ a verb.   ○ an adverb.   ○ an adjective.

24. He and his mother _____ it is a good idea.

Choose the correct word to fill the gap in the sentence.

   ○ thinks   ○ think   ○ thinking

25. Australians are _____ to refugees than people in some other countries.

Choose the correct word to fill the gap in the sentence.

   ○ kindest   ○ more kinder   ○ kind   ○ kinder

> Did you colour in one of the circles?

It would be a good idea to check your answers to questions 1 to 25 before moving on to the other questions.

To the student

Ask your teacher or parent to read the spelling words for you. The words are listed on page 167. Write the spelling words on the lines below.

Test 1 spelling words

26. _____

27. _____

28. _____

29. _____

30. _____

31. _____

32. _____

33. _____

34. _____

35. _____

36. _____

37. _____

38. _____

39. _____

40. _____

There is one spelling mistake in each sentence.
Write the correct spelling for each underlined word in the box.

41. Our restaurant is a great place for a <u>berthday</u> party.

42. Every child gets a special <u>meel</u>.

43. You get a small burger, fries, drink and a <u>serprize</u>.

44. There is also a gift to take <u>hoem</u>.

45. Children love our parties and parents do <u>to</u>.

Read the paragraph about Pokemon Island. There is one spelling mistake on each line. Write the correct spelling in the box.

46. Explaw *Pokemon Island*. Your help is

47. needed to identify the meny Pokemon that

48. live on the island. Be as quite as possible.

49. At the beech you will see Kangashkan.

50. In the tunnel you might fin Magnemite.

Did you write your answer in the box?

END OF TEST

Well done! You have completed the first Conventions of Language Test.

How did you go with these test questions? Some were harder than the sample questions. Check to see where you did well and where you had problems. Try to revise the questions that were hard for you.

Use the diagnostic chart on pages 97–98 to see which level of ability you reached. This is only an estimate. Don't be surprised if you answered some difficult questions correctly or even missed some easier questions.

There are now three more tests, each containing 50 questions. They include many of the same types of questions, plus a few new types.

An important note about the NAPLAN Online tests

The NAPLAN Online Conventions of Language test will be divided into different sections. Students will only have one opportunity to check their answers at the end of each section before proceeding to the next one. This means that after students have completed a section and moved onto the next they will not be able to check their work again. We have included reminders for students to check their work at specific points in the practice tests from now on so they become familiar with this process.

Instructions

As you check the answer for each question, mark it as correct (✓) or incorrect (✗). Mark any questions that you omitted or left out as incorrect (✗) for the moment.

Then look at how many you answered correctly in each level. You will be able to see what level you are at by finding the point where you started having consistent difficulty with questions at a certain level. For example, if you answer most questions correctly up to the Intermediate level and then get most questions wrong from then onwards, it is likely your ability is at the Intermediate level. You can ask your parents or your teacher to help you do this if it isn't clear to you.

Am I able to ...

	SKILL	ESTIMATED LEVEL	✓ or ✗
1	Insert the correct verb?	Advanced	
2	Use a question mark correctly?	Advanced	
3	Use speech marks correctly for direct speech?	Standard	
4	Use apostrophes correctly?	Standard	
5	Use apostrophes correctly?	Standard	
6	Insert the correct verb?	Standard	
7	Insert the correct verb?	Standard	
8	Recognise the correct tense?	Standard	
9	Recognise the correct tense?	Intermediate	
10	Recognise the correct tense?	Standard	
11	Use a capital letter for the start of a sentence?	Intermediate	
12	Use a pronoun correctly?	Standard	
13	Identify the correct form of an adverb?	Intermediate	
14	Insert a full stop at the end of a sentence?	Intermediate	
15	Identify the correct preposition?	Standard	
16	Use a pronoun and verb correctly?	Intermediate	
17	End a sentence with a full stop?	Advanced	
18	Identify a noun in a short sentence?	Intermediate	
19	Recognise an adjective?	Advanced	
20	Identify a pronoun in a short sentence?	Intermediate	
21	Identify a contraction?	Advanced	
22	Recognise that a proper noun requires a capital letter?	Advanced	
23	Identify a verb in a short sentence?	Advanced	
24	Use tense correctly with two pronouns?	Advanced	
25	Use a comparative adjective correctly?	Advanced	
26	Spell *poor*?	Standard	
27	Spell *kind*?	Standard	
28	Spell *most*?	Advanced	

	SKILL	ESTIMATED LEVEL	✓ or ✗
29	Spell *sold*?	Intermediate	
30	Spell *moon*?	Intermediate	
31	Spell *fast*?	Intermediate	
32	Spell *class*?	Standard	
33	Spell *football*?	Standard	
34	Spell *children*?	Standard	
35	Spell *mother*?	Standard	
36	Spell *even*?	Standard	
37	Spell *wooden*?	Standard	
38	Spell *sugar*?	Standard	
39	Spell *until*?	Standard	
40	Spell *better*?	Intermediate	
41	Spell *birthday*?	Standard	
42	Spell *meal*?	Standard	
43	Spell *surprise*?	Intermediate	
44	Spell *home*?	Intermediate	
45	Spell *too*?	Standard	
46	Spell *explore*?	Advanced	
47	Spell *many*?	Standard	
48	Spell *quiet*?	Intermediate	
49	Spell *beach*?	Standard	
50	Spell *find*?	Standard	
	TOTAL		

This is the second Conventions of Language Test. There are 50 questions.

If you aren't sure what to do, ask your teacher or your parents to help you. Don't be afraid to ask if it isn't clear to you.

Allow around 45 minutes for this test. Take a short break if necessary.

Read the text *Quiet Pony for Sale*. Each sentence has one word that is incorrect. Colour in the circle with the correct spelling.

Quiet Pony for Sale

1. hannah came with her parents to live in the small country town.

   Hannah ○   hanna ○   Hana ○

2. She had to catch the bus to school each day

   day. ○   day! ○   day; ○

3. She saw a sign while she am waiting for the bus to arrive.

   was ○   is ○   were ○

4. The sign said, Quiet pony for sale'. In the paddock was a pony.

   'Quiet ○   "Quit ○   'Quite ○

5. The pony standed still.

   stood ○   stand ○

Adapted from *Quiet Pony for Sale* by Mary Small, HBJ, 1990

Colour in the circle with the right answer.

6. Which word in this sentence is a noun?
   She likes to write with a pen.

   ○ likes   ○ write   ○ with   ○ pen

7. Which word in this sentence is used as an adjective?
   My little cousin is called Evan.

   ○ My   ○ little   ○ cousin   ○ Evan

8. Find the pronoun in this sentence.
   Jan scored her first goal yesterday.

   ○ scored   ○ her   ○ goal   ○ yesterday

Some parts are missing from the sentences below. Colour in the circle with the correct words to complete the sentence. Look also for missing commas or punctuation.

9. A butterfly comes ▮▮▮▮▮▮▮.

    ○ of an egg

    ○ from an egg

    ○ that an egg

10. ▮▮▮▮▮▮▮▮▮▮ the eggs grew into caterpillars.

    ○ The female butterfly, which was a beautiful mixture of colours, laid her eggs under a leaf and

    ○ The female butterfly which was a beautiful, mixture of colours, laid her eggs under a leaf and

    ○ The female butterfly which was a beautiful mixture of colours laid her eggs under a leaf, and

11. The teacher said, ▮▮▮▮▮▮▮▮▮

    ○ The caterpillar will attach itself to a nearby branch and begin spinning its cocoon.

    ○ "The caterpillar will attach itself to a nearby branch and begin spinning its cocoon."

    ○ The caterpillar will "attach itself to a nearby branch and begin spinning its cocoon."

12. ▮▮▮▮▮▮▮ the fully grown caterpillar shed its skin.

    ○ After a little while you and I will sees

    ○ After a little while you and I will see

    ○ After a little while you and I will seen

Did you colour in one of the circles?

Read the text below. Answer questions 13 to 17.

Most people believe that Mount Everest is the tallest mountain in the world.

Officially it is the tallest mountain in the world.

Experts say that it is not the tallest.

The peak of Everest is further above sea level than the peak of any other mountain.

Mauna Kea is the tallest from the bottom to the top.

13. Most people believe Mount Everest is the tallest mountain in the world.

Which word can be removed from this sentence and not change the meaning?

○ Most   ○ believe   ○ tallest   ○ world

14. Which sentences can be joined by *but* without changing the meaning?

○ Sentences 1 and 2   ○ Sentences 2 and 4   ○ Sentences 4 and 5

15. Experts say that it is not the tallest.

In this sentence the word *it* means

○ experts.   ○ Mauna Kea.   ○ Everest.   ○ world.

16. The peak of Everest is further above sea level than the peak of any other mountain.

The word *than* is used to

○ join.   ○ question.   ○ disagree.   ○ compare.

17. Most people believe Mount Everest is the tallest mountain in the world.

The word *believe* is

○ a noun.   ○ an adjective.   ○ an adverb.   ○ a verb.

Did you colour in one of the circles?

Answer the following questions. Colour in only one circle for each answer.

18. Which of these is a complete statement?

○ Coming to Perth

○ I will be counting.

○ Looking forward to.

○ Every Saturday

19. Which sentence is correct?

○ Its' a long time away.

○ I'ts coat was rough and covered in mud.

○ It's coat was rough and covered in mud.

○ Its coat was rough and covered in mud.

20. Which sentence is correct?

○ We are headed to sydney

○ We are headed to Adelaide.

○ we are headed to Melbourne.

21. ▢▢▢▢▢ you let them build units then we will lose our play area.

Choose the correct word to fill the gap in the sentence.

○ If   ○ As   ○ Of   ○ How

22. Which sentence is correct?

○ The sign was glued to a wall?

○ The sign was glued to a wall;

○ The sign was glued to a wall,

○ The sign was glued to a wall.

Did you colour in one of the circles?

23. He ▢▢▢▢▢ at her with sad eyes.

Choose the correct word to fill the gap in the sentence.

○ look

○ looking

○ looked

24. Which sentence is correctly punctuated?

○ "Here pony" said Hannah,

○ Here pony said Hannah,

○ "Here pony," said Hannah.

○ "Here pony said Hannah",

25. Tomorrow ████████████████ to India.

Choose the correct words to fill the gap in the sentence.

○ he was going

○ he are going

○ he will go

○ he has gone

It would be a good idea to check your answers to questions 1 to 25 before moving on to the other questions.

To the student

Ask your teacher or parent to read the spelling words for you. The words are listed on page 167. Write the spelling words on the lines below.

Test 2 spelling words

26. _____

27. _____

28. _____

29. _____

30. _____

31. _____

32. _____

33. _____

34. _____

35. _____

36. _____

37. _____

38. _____

39. _____

40. _____

Read the letter. The spelling mistakes have been underlined.
Write the correct spelling for each underlined word in the box.

Dear Mayor

41. I am writing to you about the park <u>neer</u> our school.

42. If you let them build units we will <u>loos</u> our play area.

43. Kids from the area will have <u>kno</u> play equipment to use.

44, We use that park because it is very shady and <u>pritty</u>.

45. If you let them build then many kids and <u>there</u> parents will be very angry.

From
Anthony James

There is one spelling mistake in each sentence.
Write the correct spelling of the word in the box.

46. Pleese don't let this happen.

47. It's the only one we hav.

48. My feat were hurting after that long bushwalk.

49. I had to paws the video while I went to answer the phone.

50. Roger road down the river until it became dark.

Did you write your answer in the box?

Instructions

As you check the answer for each question, mark it as correct ($\checkmark$) or incorrect ($\times$). Mark any questions that you omitted or left out as incorrect ($\times$) for the moment.

Then look at how many you answered correctly in each level. You will be able to see what level you are at by finding the point where you started having consistent difficulty with questions at a certain level. For example, if you answer most questions correctly up to the Intermediate level and then get most questions wrong from then onwards, it is likely your ability is at athe Intermediate level. You can ask your parents or your teacher to help you do this if it isn't clear to you.

Am I able to ...

	SKILL	ESTIMATED LEVEL	$\checkmark$ or $\times$
1	Use capital letters for proper nouns?	Intermediate	
2	Use a full stop correctly?	Intermediate	
3	Use the past tense correctly?	Intermediate	
4	Use quotation marks?	Standard	
5	Use the irregular past tense correctly?	Standard	
6	Identify a noun in a short sentence?	Standard	
7	Recognise an adjective?	Intermediate	
8	Identify a pronoun in a short sentence?	Intermediate	
9	Identify the correct preposition?	Standard	
10	Place commas correctly?	Advanced	
11	Use speech marks correctly for direct speech?	Standard	
12	Use tense correctly with a pronoun?	Intermediate	
13	Remove a word without changing the meaning?	Advanced	
14	Use a conjunction?	Advanced	
15	Identify the word related to a pronoun?	Advanced	
16	Know how a preposition is used to compare?	Advanced	
17	Identify a verb?	Intermediate	
18	Make a complete statement?	Intermediate	
19	Identify the correct word?	Intermediate	
20	Use correct punctuation in a short sentence?	Intermediate	
21	Use a conjunction to introduce a clause?	Advanced	
22	Use correct punctuation in a short sentence?	Intermediate	
23	Use a verb to compete a sentence?	Intermediate	
24	Use correct punctuation in a short sentence?	Advanced	
25	Use a verb to complete a sentence?	Advanced	
26	Spell *door*?	Intermediate	
27	Spell *old*?	Standard	

	SKILL	ESTIMATED LEVEL	✓ or ✗
28	Spell *pink?*	Intermediate	
29	Spell *mind?*	Intermediate	
30	Spell *lost?*	Advanced	
31	Spell *soon?*	Intermediate	
32	Spell *plant?*	Intermediate	
33	Spell *bath?*	Standard	
34	Spell *last?*	Intermediate	
35	Spell *brother?*	Intermediate	
36	Spell *great?*	Standard	
37	Spell *many?*	Standard	
38	Spell *people?*	Intermediate	
39	Spell *money?*	Intermediate	
40	Spell *climb?*	Standard	
41	Spell *near?*	Intermediate	
42	Spell *lose?*	Standard	
43	Spell *no?*	Intermediate	
44	Spell *pretty?*	Intermediate	
45	Spell *their?*	Standard	
46	Spell *please?*	Intermediate	
47	Spell *have?*	Standard	
48	Spell *feet?*	Intermediate	
49	Spell *pause?*	Intermediate	
50	Spell *rowed?*	Intermediate	
	TOTAL		

CONVENTIONS OF LANGUAGE TEST 3

ADAPTED FOR
ONLINE
FORMAT

This is the third Conventions of Language Test. There are 50 questions.

If you aren't sure what to do, ask your teacher or your parents to help you. Don't be afraid to ask if it isn't clear to you.

Allow around 45 minutes for this test. Take a short break if necessary.

Each sentence has one word that is incorrect. Choose the correct word for the sentence. Colour in the circle with the correct answer.

1. they were very angry.

   ○ They   ○ they   ○ wer   ○ angry

2. He are playing in the school band.

   ○ am   ○ will   ○ he   ○ is

3. My dad was born in perth, Western Australia.

   ○ western   ○ is   ○ Perth   ○ borne

4. He listened too each student say their speech.

   ○ there   ○ speach   ○ listen   ○ to

5. My mother and me went to the shopping mall.

   ○ us   ○ shoping   ○ too   ○ I

Read the sentences and choose the correct word or words to complete them. Colour in one circle for each answer.

6. Nicholas and Mary-Ellen _____ cousins.

is	are	was
○	○	○

7. Anthony _____ John are brothers.

or	and	with
○	○	○

8. Angelena used to live at _____ .

   ○ 17 edward Avenue
   ○ 17 Edward avenue
   ○ 17 Edward Avenue

9. John's school was _____ .

   ○ Waverley College at Bondi
   ○ Waverley college at Bondi
   ○ waverley college at bondi

Colour in the circle with the right answer.

10. Which word in this sentence is a noun?
The bus stopped suddenly.

○ The   ○ bus

○ stopped   ○ suddenly

11 Which word in this sentence is used as an adjective?
We saw a funny movie yesterday.

○ We

○ funny

○ movie

○ yesterday

12. Which word in this sentence is a pronoun?
Some teachers care about how we feel at school.

○ Some

○ about

○ how

○ we

Read the sentences. Three words are underlined. Only one is correct.
Circle the correct word or punctuation.

13. Food from plants can give us energy **and / but / if** keep us healthy.

14. Food can also be sweet just **four / for / fore** taste.

15. **Us / Our / We** use sugar made from sugarcane to make some food sweet.

16. There are many animals such as birds **. / ? / ,** bees and bears that like sweet food.

17. Many drinks **are / is / am** made using plants.

18. Coffee and tea both come **of / to / from** plants.

Read the sentences. They have some gaps. Choose the correct word to fill the gap. Colour in one circle for each answer.

19. Here are the ▨▨▨ you will need.

thing ○   things ○

20. There ▨▨▨ a line that is drawn in red.

am ○   be ○   is ○   are ○

21. There ▨▨▨ about ten girls in that class.

is ○   are ○

22. Use a compass to work out ▨▨▨ way is north.

the ○   which ○   how ○   that ○

23. Here is a photo ▨▨▨ the team.

over ○   off ○   of ○

24. In French the word *gare* ▨▨▨ station.

means ○   railway ○   be ○   English ○

25. Sign the sheet to prove that ▨▨▨ been at each game.

you've ○   you ○

Did you colour in one of the circles?

It would be a good idea to check your answers to questions 1 to 25 before moving on to the other questions.

109

☞ **Answers and explanations on page 164**

To the student

Ask your teacher or parent to read the spelling words for you. The words are listed on page 168. Write the spelling words on the lines below.

Test 3 spelling words

26. _____   34. _____

27. _____   35. _____

28. _____   36. _____

29. _____   37. _____

30. _____   38. _____

31. _____   39. _____

32. _____   40. _____

33. _____

Read the text *Amphibians*. The words that are underlined are spelling mistakes. Write the correct spelling for each underlined word in the box.

Amphibians

Amphibians are animals that live on land

41. sum of the time, and in water the

rest of the time. Frogs are amphibians.

A frog's skin is **42.** smoothe and moist. In spring,

frogs lay their eggs in the **43.** worter. The eggs hatch

into tadpoles. They have long **44.** tales to swim with.

As they get **45.** bigga, tadpoles grow legs and turn into frogs.

Each sentence has one word that is incorrect. Write the correct spelling of the word in the box.

46. Squirrels are not founed in Australia.

47. Squirrels live in other countrys.

48. They run allong branches.

49. They serch the ground for food.

50. Squirrels bery nuts in the ground.

Did you write your answer in the box?

END OF TEST

Well done! You have completed the third Conventions of Language Test.

How did you go with these test questions? Some were harder than the last test. Check to see where you did well and where you had problems. Try to revise the questions that were hard for you.

Use the diagnostic chart on pages 112–113 to see which level of ability you reached. Again, we remind you that this is only an estimate. Don't be surprised if you answered some difficult questions correctly or even missed some easier questions.

There is now only one more test to complete. It contains 50 questions. They include many of the same types of questions, plus a few new types.

Instructions

As you check the answer for each question, mark it as correct (✓) or incorrect (✖). Mark any questions that you omitted or left out as incorrect (✖) for the moment.

Then look at how many you answered correctly in each level. You will be able to see what level you are at by finding the point where you started having consistent difficulty with questions at a certain level. For example, if you answer most questions correctly up to the Intermediate level and then get most questions wrong from then onwards, it is likely your ability is at the Intermediatee level. You can ask your parents or your teacher to help you do this if it isn't clear to you.

Am I able to ...

	SKILL	ESTIMATED LEVEL	✓ or ✖
1	Commence a sentence with a capital letter?	Standard	
2	Use the correct verb?	Standard	
3	Use a capital letter for a proper noun?	Intermediate	
4	Use the appropriate preposition?	Intermediate	
5	Use the correct pronoun?	Intermediate	
6	Use correct tense with a pronoun?	Standard	
7	Recognise common grammatical convention (conjunction)?	Intermediate	
8	Use capital letters for proper nouns?	Intermediate	
9	Use capital letters for proper nouns?	Advanced	
10	Identify a noun?	Intermediate	
11	Identify an adjective?	Intermediate	
12	Identify a pronoun?	Intermediate	
13	Recognise common grammatical convention (conjunction)?	Intermediate	
14	Use a preposition correctly and spell a common one-syllable word?	Advanced	
15	Correctly use a pronoun?	Intermediate	
16	Correctly place commas for punctuation?	Intermediate	
17	Correctly use tense?	Standard	
18	Identify the correct preposition from three alternatives?	Advanced	
19	Correctly use a plural noun?	Advanced	
20	Use correct tense?	Intermediate	
21	Identify the correct verb?	Standard	
22	Select a pronoun?	Advanced	
23	Use a preposition correctly?	Advanced	
24	Spell a frequently used word and correctly use tense?	Advanced	
25	Correctly use pronoun and a contraction?	Advanced	
26	Spell *floor*?	Standard	
27	Spell *find*?	Standard	

	SKILL	ESTIMATED LEVEL	✓ or ✗
28	Spell *book?*	Intermediate	
29	Spell *tree?*	Standard	
30	Spell *gold?*	Advanced	
31	Spell *path?*	Standard	
32	Spell *past?*	Standard	
33	Spell *boat?*	Standard	
34	Spell *pretty?*	Intermediate	
35	Spell *father?*	Standard	
36	Spell *finger?*	Intermediate	
37	Spell *could?*	Standard	
38	Spell *today?*	Standard	
39	Spell *begin?*	Intermediate	
40	Spell *visit?*	Standard	
41	Spell a common word?	Intermediate	
42	Spell a one-syllable word?	Standard	
43	Spell a frequently used word?	Standard	
44	Spell a common word with a less regular pattern?	Intermediate	
45	Spell a common word?	Intermediate	
46	Spell a one-syllable word?	Intermediate	
47	Spell a common word with a less regular pattern?	Standard	
48	Spell a common word?	Intermediate	
49	Spell a less frequently used word?	Standard	
50	Spell a common word with a less regular pattern?	Intermediate	
	TOTAL		

ADAPTED FOR
ONLINE
FORMAT

This is the last Conventions of Language Test. There are 50 questions.

If you aren't sure what to do, ask your teacher or your parents to help you. Don't be afraid to ask if it isn't clear to you.

Allow around 45 minutes for this test. Take a short break if necessary.

Read the sentences. Choose the correct word or words to complete them. Colour in one circle for each answer.

1. Everyone _____ there was a ghost in the story.

   knew   knowed   known
   ○   ○   ○

2. They liked the _____ game of cricket.

   once   first
   ○   ○

3. _____ house was the most decorated house in the street at Christmas time.

   Gerry's   Gerrys   Gerries
   ○   ○   ○

4. _____ was a dangerous place to swim.

   It   it
   ○   ○

The mistakes in these sentences have been underlined. Colour in the circle with the correct answer.

5. miss good is our neighbour.

   ○ Miss good
   ○ Miss Good
   ○ Miss good

   Did you colour in one of the circles?

6. There are six horses in Mr Teds stables.

   Teds'   Ted's
   ○   ○

7. He always comes two our house.

   that   to   it
   ○   ○   ○

8. she was tall.

   They   She   Her
   ○   ○   ○

Colour in the circle with the right answer.

9 Which word in this sentence is a noun?
He painted the wooden door carefully

He   painted   wooden   door
○   ○   ○   ○

10. Which word in this sentence is used as an adjective?
The early bus to Marrickville will get me home.

early   bus   get   home
○   ○   ○   ○

11. Which words can replace the pronoun *they* in this sentence?
Nicholas said they will play cricket on Saturday.

Nicholas and I   my coach   Sam and me   my friends
○   ○   ○   ○

Read the passage. It has some gaps. Choose the correct word to fill the gaps.
Colour in the circle with the correct answer.

12. Mary and Anthony stepped ⬚ the boat.

	into	under	through
	○	○	○

13. We took the lifejackets ⬚ put them on.

	and	for	so
	○	○	○

14. Mary used an oar ⬚ push away from the wharf.

	to	for	as
	○	○	○

15. She gave a signal to her dad and the boat took ⬚.

	off	on	in
	○	○	○

16. Shade three circles to show which words should start with a capital letter.

The early australian sports were a mixture of those from england and ireland.

17. Where does the missing full stop (**.**) go?

Australia plays all sports Australia is a world leader in swimming.

18. Colour in one circle to show where the missing full stop (**.**) should go.

Sport is   something to be enjoyed   by everyone   It is fun and enjoyable.

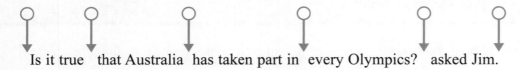

19. Colour in **two** circles to show where the speech marks (**"** and **"**) should go.

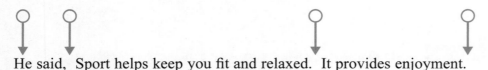

Is it true   that Australia has taken part in every Olympics?   asked Jim.

20. Where should the missing speech marks (**"** and **"**) go?

He said, Sport helps keep you fit and relaxed. It provides enjoyment.

Adapted from *Sport in the Making: A History of Popular Sport in Australia* by Shane Power, HBJ, 1990

CONVENTIONS OF LANGUAGE TEST 4

Read the sentences and choose the correct word or words to complete them. Colour in one circle for each answer.

21. Nick and Leo ________ fish for lunch.

- ○ is eating
- ○ are eating
- ○ will eating

22. Jim is ________ father.

- ○ Anthonys
- ○ Anthony's
- ○ Anthonys'

23. Max, who is a teacher ________ used to live in Maroubra.

,	.	?	!
○	○	○	○

24. John said that his sore leg is ________ .

better	gooder	bestest
○	○	○

25. Peter is the ________ in the family.

- ○ tallest
- ○ most tallest
- ○ more tallest

It would be a good idea to check your answers to questions 1 to 25 before moving on to the other questions.

To the student

Ask your teacher or parent to read the spelling words for you. The words are listed on page 168. Write the spelling words on the lines below.

Test 4 spelling words

26. _____

27. _____

28. _____

29. _____

30. _____

31. _____

32. _____

33. _____

34. _____

35. _____

36. _____

37. _____

38. _____

39. _____

40. _____

**Read the sentences. The spelling mistakes have been underlined.
Write the correct spelling of the word in the box.**

Your backyard is a miniature <u>jungel</u>.　　　　　41. ☐

Little creatures hide among the plants and lurk <u>unda</u> leaves.　　　42. ☐

Insects and plants <u>deepend</u> on each other for survival.　　　43. ☐

Plants <u>provid</u> animals with oxygen, food and shelter.　　　44. ☐

Animals help plants by <u>spreding</u> their pollen or seeds.　　　45. ☐

Each sentence has one word that is incorrect.
Write the correct spelling of the word in the box.

There are many inhabitents in your garden.   46.

A few are very tyni.   47.

These can only be seen using a magnafying glass.   46.

There are many insects and most can be seen with the nakid eye.   49.

You need to no where and when to look for them.   50.

Adapted from *Your Backyard Jungle* by Kerri Bingle,
David Bowden & Jenny Dibley, HBJ, 1992.

END OF TEST

Well done! You have completed the final Conventions of Language Test. It means that you have answered or attempted 200 Conventions of Language questions.

How did you go with the questions in this test? Were some harder for you? Check to see where you did well and where you had problems.

Use the diagnostic chart on pages 120–121 to see which level of ability you reached. Again, we remind you that this is only an estimate. Don't be surprised if you answered some difficult questions correctly or even missed some easier questions.

Instructions

As you check the answer for each question, mark it as correct (✓) or incorrect (✗). Mark any questions that you omitted or left out as incorrect (✗) for the moment.

Then look at how many you answered correctly in each level. You will be able to see what level you are at by finding the point where you started having consistent difficulty with questions at a certain level. For example, if you answer most questions correctly up to the Intermediate level and then get most questions wrong from then onwards, it is likely your ability is at the Intermediate level. You can ask your parents or your teacher to help you do this if it isn't clear to you.

Am I able to ...

	SKILL	ESTIMATED LEVEL	✓ or ✗
1	Correctly use tense?	Intermediate	
2	Use an adjective correctly?	Standard	
3	Use an apostrophe?	Intermediate	
4	Recognise a basic grammatical convention (start a sentence with a capital letter)?	Standard	
5	Use capital letters for proper nouns?	Standard	
6	Use an apostrophe?	Intermediate	
7	Use a preposition correctly?	Standard	
8	Recognise a basic grammatical convention (starts a sentence with a capital letter) ?	Standard	
9	Identify a noun?	Advanced	
10	Identify an adjective?	Advanced	
11	Replace a pronoun?	Intermediate	
12	Identify the correct preposition?	Intermediate	
13	Identify the correct conjunction?	Intermediate	
14	Identify the correct preposition?	Standard	
15	Identify the correct preposition?	Intermediate	
16	Use capital letters for proper nouns?	Advanced	
17	Recognise a basic grammatical convention (use of a full stop) ?	Intermediate	
18	Recognise a basic grammatical convention (use of a full stop) ?	Advanced	
19	Correctly use speech marks for direct speech?	Advanced	
20	Correctly use speech marks for direct speech?	Advanced	
21	Correctly use tense with a pronoun?	Advanced	
22	Correctly use an apostrophe?	Intermediate	
23	Correctly place commas for punctuation?	Advanced	
24	Correctly use a comparative adverb?	Advanced	
25	Correctly use a superlative adjective?	Advanced	

	SKILL	ESTIMATED LEVEL	✓ or ✗
26	Spell *sat*?	Intermediate	
27	Spell *look*?	Intermediate	
28	Spell *home*?	Intermediate	
29	Spell *land*?	Intermediate	
30	Spell *hold*?	Intermediate	
31	Spell *felt*?	Standard	
32	Spell *grass*?	Intermediate	
33	Spell *road*?	Intermediate	
34	Spell *behind*?	Standard	
35	Spell *children*?	Standard	
36	Spell *sister*?	Intermediate	
37	Spell *should*?	Advanced	
38	Spell *crowd*?	Advanced	
39	Spell *shake*?	Intermediate	
40	Spell *thinking*?	Intermediate	
41	Spell *jungle*?	Intermediate	
42	Spell *under*?	Standard	
43	Spell *depend*?	Intermediate	
44	Spell *provide*?	Advanced	
45	Spell *spreading*?	Advanced	
46	Spell *inhabitants*?	Advanced	
47	Spell *tiny*?	Intermediate	
48	Spell *magnifying*?	Intermediate	
49	Spell *naked*?	Intermediate	
50	Spell *know*?	Intermediate	
	TOTAL		

Check the Writing section (www.nap. edu.au/naplan/writing) **of the official NAPLAN website for up-to-date and important information on the Writing Test.** Sample Writing Tests and marking guidelines that outline the criteria markers use when assessing your writing are also provided. Please note that, to date in NAPLAN, the types of texts that students have been tested on have been narrative and persuasive writing.

The Australian Curriculum for English requires students to be taught three main types of texts:

- imaginative writing (including narratives and descriptions)
- informative writing (including procedures and reports)
- persuasive writing (expositions).

Informative writing has not yet been tested by NAPLAN. The best preparation for writing is for students to read a range of texts and to get lots of practice in writing different types of texts. We have included information on all types of texts in this book.

About the test

The NAPLAN Writing Test examines a student's ability to write effectively in a specific type of text. Students will come across a number of types of texts at school. These can be factual (real) or literary (imaginary). Although we provide you with some graded sample answers on pages 126–127 and 140–141, we do not provide any others because grading writing is a time-consuming task which can be very subjective. It's more important that you focus on improving the standard of your writing.

Usually there is only one Writing question in the NAPLAN Writing Test. You will be provided with some stimulus material that acts as a prompt to writing: something to read or a picture to look at.

The NAPLAN Online Writing Test

For the Year 3 NAPLAN Writing Test, unlike the other year levels, students will not use a digital device (a computer or tablet); they will write their answer on paper.

Marking the Writing Test

When the markers of the NAPLAN Writing Test assess your writing they will mark it according to various criteria. Knowing what they look for will help you understand what to look out for in your own writing.

The emphasis is on the quality of expression and what the student has to say. Some features that may be emphasised are:

- the quality of the content
- what the student thinks about the topic
- what feelings are developed
- how it is structured
- whether the writing is organised clearly, using paragraphs and appropriate sequencing
- whether the writing is cohesive
- the quality of the spelling and punctuation/ grammar.

Advice for parents and teachers

If students aren't sure how to write a persuasive or narrative text then use the practice tests to develop these skills. It may not be easy for them at first. One way to start is to ask them to talk about the topic and to state their views on the subject. Next you could show them how to plan their writing. Then they can start to write.

Give plenty of praise and encouragement. Remember that Year 3 students are still quite young. Emphasise whatever is good and overlook any errors at first. Space out the time between the writing tasks. Do not attempt one immediately after the other as this does not allow time for development. Come back to these errors at a much later stage, perhaps a little before you start the next practice test.

In this book we look at persuasive and narrative writing. We start with writing a persuasive text on the following page.

WRITING: PERSUASIVE TEXTS

In this section we start with a sample of a persuasive text. First we give some details about this type of writing, then there is a sample question with answers, and finally there are two practice Writing Tests for persuasive texts.

About persuasive texts

- A persuasive text is designed to convince. It states one side of a case and expresses a point of view. The first step is to decide on your opinion: are you for or against?

- You don't need to list reasons for and reasons against. Support your point of view with facts, examples and evidence.

- Persuasive texts can be posters, advertisements, letters, debates or reports.

- Their main purpose is to persuade the reader to see an issue from the author's point of view. The writing aims to persuade the reader to change his or her mind, and to win the support of the reader on a specific issue. To do this the author uses persuasive devices.

Examples of persuasive devices

- You can speak to the reader.
  For example:
  The government should give money to countries that suffer from famine and disasters. This will show that Australia cares for all people that suffer. It is important that we all donate to foreign aid charities.

- You can ask a question that leads to the answer you want.
  For example:
  Students are able to judge just as fairly as adults. So isn't it right to let them have a say in some matters?

- You can give facts and support your ideas with findings.
  For example:
  The majority of scientists at the world conference agreed on climate change.

- You can use descriptive persuasive words.
  For example:
  true, fair, honest, essential, best.

- You can use persuasive words to influence the reader.
  For example:
  naturally, obviously, definitely, probably, certainly.

- You can use strong modal verbs.
  For example:
  can, might, should, could, would.

- You can use words that make the reader think. Thinking words can include persuasive statistics.
  For example:
  90% of children are eating too much salt.

- You can include emotional language.
  For example:
  Many people consider that ..., We must protect ..., Certainly we must try ..., I am absolutely appalled that ...

- You can use emotional adjectives.
  For example:
  important, significant, invaluable.

- You can use rhetorical questions. A rhetorical question asks the reader a question but does not expect an answer. It is used for its persuasive effect. It makes the reader think and tries to emphasise one likely answer.
  For example:
  Are we to think that ...?

Structure of a persuasive text

Introduction

- The first paragraph introduces the topic. Make this a statement of your opinion.

- It should be a short paragraph of approximately one to two sentences. It should include a strong sentence which captures the reader's interest.

The body

The main part of your writing should consist of arguments. In a persuasive text an argument shows how you think by listing the reasons for your opinion. It is the case that you are putting forward, just like a lawyer puts forward a case in court. Focus on the main points and elaborate on them.

- Use a new paragraph for each new point or idea. Include reasons, evidence and examples to support your opinion.

- Try to include at least three paragraphs with at least two sentences in each paragraph. Avoid using paragraphs of one sentence only.

- State your arguments or ideas in order, one after the other. They should be logical, i.e. they should make sense. Start with the strongest argument.

- Express your point of view clearly. Use strong, persuasive language. Back up each idea, opinion or argument with evidence.

- Use linking words. Linking words are sometimes called connectives. Connectives are words that improve the flow of your writing and are used to join ideas.
  For example:
  firstly, secondly, thirdly, another reason, finally, because, next, then, when, after, so, therefore, however, even though, for this reason, although, pay attention to, another point of view, on the other hand, alternatively.

- Use the present tense to explain ideas or arguments.
  For example:
  I believe that ...

- Use the past tense to give examples.
  For example:
  I have heard that ..., People have tried to ...

- Remember to acknowledge your sources when you use information or statistics. In other words, give the reader an idea of where the facts were obtained.

Conclusion

The conclusion is a strong, convincing statement used to repeat your position and summarise all your key points.

For example:

In conclusion, it is evident that ...

It does not contain any new information or points. The conclusion should be about three sentences in length.

On the following page we have provided a Sample Writing question for a persuasive text. In the persuasive text you will be required to:

- express an opinion
- include facts to support your opinion
- make sure that the first sentence of each paragraph is the key to what follows
- write in an easy-to-understand way
- persuade the reader
- use a new paragraph for each new idea.

We have also provided three sample answers to the sample question. We have grouped them into the three levels of ability used throughout this book. Please note that these are approximate guidelines only.

SAMPLE QUESTION: PERSUASIVE WRITING

In this part you will be doing some writing. Each Writing Test should take you 40 minutes. Write your answer on separate sheets of paper. Use the top part of the first sheet or the persuasive text planning page to plan your ideas.

When you have finished, hand in your writing to your teacher, parents or another adult to mark it for you.

Topic: Should we be allowed to have native animals as pets?

Today you are going to write a persuasive text. The topic for your writing is whether we should be allowed to have native animals as pets.

Write an answer that shows your opinion and ideas.

- Begin with a clear opening paragraph: tell the reader what you are going to write.
- Then write your opinions.
- Give your reasons: be convincing.
- Explain so that someone else can understand easily.
- At the end give a short summary of your ideas.

Remember to:

- think about your views on the topic
- include a clear opening and concluding statement
- plan your writing, thinking about arguments for and against
- use paragraphs
- write in sentences
- check your spelling and punctuation
- write at least one page.

SAMPLE ANSWERS: PERSUASIVE WRITING

Should we be allowed to have native animals as pets?

STANDARD LEVEL 1

animals has a hom

I take the animal to my houm

animals not hapy

To bad want to com stay in my houm.

STANDARD LEVEL 2

Animals not good for pets.

First will rek them

and will liv not hapy with them

And will skwshthem in our homs

And have dezees.

THE END

INTERMEDIATE LEVEL 1

Native animals as pets is a really silly idea.

The first reason is that you take them from their homes

The second reason is that they are not with other animals.

Another reason is it can hurt them.

Remember animals belong in the bush and not in our homes.

INTERMEDIATE LEVEL 2

Native animals would not be good as pets. We should leave them where they belong.

Firstly animals are not always as cute as you first think. They can grow big quite quickly and can die quickly if you don't help them.

Secondly, taking animals away from other animals makes them lonely. Taking them from their homes is too far away so they won't be able to go back and visit. So, we shouldn't kidnap them.

Thirdly, animals need somewhere to relax and refresh their brains so don't destroy their homes.

Next, they won't have company and won't produce so numbers of animals will go down or disappear altogether.

Finally, animals are not that easy to look after. Don't think that they are cute and cuddly and don't need lots of work. You can't just let them free like in the bush.

In conclusion, I believe animals as pets should be banned.

Please note: Spelling, punctuation and grammar errors have been included to replicate the likely response of a Year 3 student.

SAMPLE ANSWERS: PERSUASIVE WRITING

ADVANCED LEVEL 1

Native animals would not be good as pets although it may sound like a good idea. There are lots of reasons why.

Firstly, taking these cute animals away from their natural environment will lead to extinction. Animals such as the bilby, the wombat and the koala live in the Australian bush. Taking them away from their home is like keeping an animal prisoner. If we take them, it would not be with others of its kind, so then it couldn't mate. That would cause the animal numbers to go down or disappear altogether. Scientists state that there are well over 5,000 species of endangered or animals and birds on our planet. Do you want to contribute to that?

Secondly, having a native animal as a pet can be dangerous, especially once they grow bigger. Some become very hard to manage because they are not used to living squashed in cages.

Finally having animals as pet stops them from acting naturally . You can't let them free like in the bush. They become frustrated and bored.

Therefore I believe that animals should stay in their homes, not ours- it's much safer for everyone and allows them to act normally and naturally.

ADVANCED LEVEL 2

Native animals would not be good as pets although it may sound like a good idea. We desperately need to keep them in their homes and not kidnap them purely for our benefit.

Firstly, taking these cute and cuddly animals away from their natural environment could lead to mass extinction. It's destroying an animals way of life. It's like keeping an animal prisoner. If you take animals in danger of extinction, you will create extinction. The Australian Bureau of Statistics states that since European settlement, over 200 years ago, 18 species of mammals have become extinct.

In addition, some native animals such as the bilby, the wombat and the koala habitat is in the Australian bush. It would not be with others of its kind. With it not being with others of its kind it wouldn't mate. That would cause the animal numbers to go down

Despite what some may think, those cute cuddly native animals are not easy to look after especially once they grow bigger. Some become sick or can die because we are unable to give them the care they require.

Lastly, some become very hard to manage because they are not used to living squashed in a cage. They become bored and stressed. They could even become dangerous to children they are living with.

Also, we don't know what diseases these native animals could spread to us.

Finally, as cities grow and habitats for animals no longer exist, taking them from their homes is like kidnapping them. Could you live with yourself after doing such a horrible thing?

In conclusion, it's evident that native animals don't have appeal as pets. Letting native animals into our homes is just trouble: people and animals will suffer the consequences. Let's take responsibility and reverse the rate of extinction.

Please note: Spelling, punctuation and grammar errors have been included to replicate the likely response of a Year 3 student.

In this part you will be doing some writing. Each Writing Test should take you 40 minutes. Write your answer on separate sheets of paper. Use the top part of the first sheet or the persuasive text planning page to plan your ideas.

When you have finished, hand in your writing to your teacher, parents or another adult to mark it for you.

Topic: All children should have a mobile phone.

Some parents give mobile phones to their children in order to keep in contact. A mobile can be used to call for help when there is a problem. Children also like mobiles because they can talk to their friends.

Some parents refuse to give mobiles to their children because they think that they are unnecessary. Others are worried that using mobile phones can cause damage to children's brains.

What do you think? Perhaps you have some other ideas for or against giving mobile phones to children.

Write an answer that shows your opinion and ideas.

- Begin with a clear opening paragraph: tell the reader what you are going to write.

- Then write your opinions.

- Give your reasons: be convincing.

- Explain so that someone else can understand easily.

- At the end give a short summary of your ideas.

Remember to:

- think about your views on the topic

- include a clear opening and concluding statement

- plan your writing, thinking about arguments for and against

- use paragraphs

- write in sentences

- check your spelling and punctuation

- write at least one page.

Here is a persuasive text planning page to start you off. Use this page to plan your ideas.

PERSUASIVE TEXT

INTRODUCTION

Introduce the topic and state your opinion. What do you think about the issue? Are you for or against?
(1–2 sentences)

ARGUMENTS

List the reasons that support your opinion. (3–4 paragraphs)

REASON 1

List points and give examples to back up your reasons.

REASON 2

List points and give examples to back up your reasons.

REASON 3

List points and give examples to back up your reasons.

LINKING WORDS

although ... even though ... however ... on the other hand ... at the same time ...

MODAL VERBS

must ... can ... might ... should ... could ... would

PERSUASIVE WORDS

naturally ... obviously ... definitely ... probably ... certainly ... possibly ... always ... if ... unless ... sometimes ... unlikely ... hopefully ... perhaps ... absolutely ...

THINKING WORDS

Experts believe that ... It can be said that ... In my view ... Another point of view is ... The evidence supports ... In my opinion ... Some people feel ... On the other hand ... Surely ...

CONCLUSION

Repeat your opinion and summarise the main points of the argument. (3 sentences)

In conclusion ... Therefore ... I believe that ... It's evident that ... Overall ... Although there are many benefits to/in ... As a result ... In considering these arguments ...

Use this chart to evaluate your writing.

GUIDELINES FOR WRITING A PERSUASIVE TEXT	✓ or ✗
Have you clearly expressed your point of view on the specific issue?	
Have you made at least three points with strong arguments and solid supporting points?	
Have you backed up each argument with evidence?	
Have you used the simple present tense to give views, e.g. *We must try …*?	
Have you used the present perfect tense to give examples, e.g. *I have heard that …, People have tried to …*?	
Have you used a variety of correct sentence structures—including simple, compound and complex sentences—to develop arguments?	
Have you linked arguments by using a variety of time connectives, e.g. *firstly, secondly, thirdly, finally, because, in addition, next, then, when, after, consequently, so, therefore, furthermore, however, even though, for this reason, although, pay attention to, in contrast, another point of view, in spite of this, on the other hand, alternatively, the evidence supports a different point of view …*?	
Have you used clear, descriptive and persuasive words?	
Have you used modal verbs/conditionals, e.g. (high) *always, undoubtedly, certainly, absolutely, definitely, obviously, never, must*; (medium) *probably, maybe, apparently, often, can, might, should, could, would, if, unless*; (low) *unlikely, hopefully, perhaps, sometimes, possibly*?	
Have you used persuasive devices such as statistics (e.g. *75% of students in my class have a mobile phone and believe that …*), emotive language (e.g. *Many people consider that …, We must protect …, Certainly we must try …, I am absolutely appalled that …, important, significant, invaluable*) and rhetorical questions (e.g. *Are we to think that …?*)?	
Have you considered the audience and purpose of the text?	
Have you organised your writing into new paragraphs for each separate idea or argument?	
Have you used thinking and action verbs to build arguments, e.g. *In my opinion …, Some people feel …, On the other hand …, Probably …, It is certain …, Surely …*?	
Have you used a variety of conjunctions, e.g. *when, because, so, if, but, because*?	
Have you used reported speech, e.g. *'I've noticed that …', 'I've heard that …'*)?	
Have you punctuated sentences correctly with capital letters, full stops, commas, exclamation marks and question marks?	
Have you used the following correctly most of the time: speech marks, possessive apostrophes, dashes, colons, semicolons and parentheses?	
Have you used the correct spelling of common words?	
Have you used the correct spelling of unusual or difficult words?	
Have you provided an effective and convincing concluding statement that summarises your opinion, introduced by an appropriate phrase, e.g. *Consequently …, Admittedly …, In conclusion …, It's evident that …, Overall …, In considering these arguments …*?	

In this part you will be doing some writing. Each Writing Test should take you 40 minutes. Write your answer on separate sheets of paper. Use the top part of the first sheet or the persuasive text planning page to plan your ideas.

When you have finished, hand in your writing to your teacher, parents or another adult to mark it for you.

Topic: Nicola should eat breakfast cereal.

Today you are going to write a persuasive text. Nicola and Eva are arguing over what to have for breakfast. Nicola wants to eat bacon and eggs, but Eva wants to eat cereal. Imagine you are Eva. What will you say to Nicola to try to convince her to eat cereal instead?

Write an answer that shows your opinion and ideas.

- Begin with a clear opening paragraph: tell the reader what you are going to write.
- Then write your opinions.
- Give your reasons: be convincing.
- Explain so that someone else can understand easily.
- At the end give a short summary of your ideas.

Remember to:

- think about your views on the topic
- include a clear opening and concluding statement
- plan your writing, thinking about arguments for and against
- use paragraphs
- write in sentences
- check your spelling and punctuation
- write at least one page.

Use this persuasive text planning page to plan your ideas.

PERSUASIVE TEXT

INTRODUCTION

Introduce the topic and state your opinion. What do you think about the issue? Are you for or against?
(1–2 sentences)

ARGUMENTS

List the reasons that support your opinion. (3–4 paragraphs)

REASON 1

List points and give examples to back up your reasons.

REASON 2

List points and give examples to back up your reasons.

REASON 3

List points and give examples to back up your reasons.

LINKING WORDS

although ... even though ... however ... on the other hand ... at the same time ...

PERSUASIVE WORDS

naturally ... obviously ... definitely ... probably ... certainly ... possibly ... always ... if ... unless ... sometimes ... unlikely ... hopefully ... perhaps ... absolutely ...

THINKING WORDS

Experts believe that ... It can be said that ... In my view ... Another point of view is ... The evidence supports ... In my opinion ... Some people feel ... On the other hand ... Surely ...

MODAL VERBS

must ... can ... might ... should ... could ... would

CONCLUSION

Repeat your opinion and summarise the main points of the argument. (3 sentences)

In conclusion ... Therefore ... I believe that ... It's evident that ... Overall ... Although there are many benefits to/in ... As a result ... In considering these arguments ...

CHECK YOUR SKILLS: WRITING TEST 2

Use this chart to evaluate your writing.

GUIDELINES FOR WRITING A PERSUASIVE TEXT	✓ or ✗
Have you clearly expressed your point of view on the specific issue?	
Have you made at least three points with strong arguments and solid supporting points?	
Have you backed up each argument with evidence?	
Have you used the simple present tense to give views, e.g. *We must try …*?	
Have you used the present perfect tense to give examples, e.g. *I have heard that …, People have tried to …*?	
Have you used a variety of correct sentence structures—including simple, compound and complex sentences—to develop arguments?	
Have you linked arguments by using a variety of time connectives, e.g. *firstly, secondly, thirdly, finally, because, in addition, next, then, when, after, consequently, so, therefore, furthermore, however, even though, for this reason, although, pay attention to, in contrast, another point of view, in spite of this, on the other hand, alternatively, the evidence supports a different point of view …*?	
Have you used clear, descriptive and persuasive words?	
Have you used modal verbs/conditionals, e.g. (high) *always, undoubtedly, certainly, absolutely, definitely, obviously, never, must*; (medium) *probably, maybe, apparently, often, can, might, should, could, would, if, unless*; (low) *unlikely, hopefully, perhaps, sometimes, possibly*?	
Have you used persuasive devices such as statistics (e.g. *75% of students in my class have a mobile phone and believe that …*), emotive language (e.g. *Many people consider that …, We must protect …, Certainly we must try …, I am absolutely appalled that …, important, significant, invaluable*) and rhetorical questions (e.g. *Are we to think that …?*)?	
Have you considered the audience and purpose of the text?	
Have you organised your writing into new paragraphs for each separate idea or argument?	
Have you used thinking and action verbs to build arguments, e.g. *In my opinion …, Some people feel …, On the other hand …, Probably …, It is certain …, Surely …*?	
Have you used a variety of conjunctions, e.g. *when, because, so, if, but, because*?	
Have you used reported speech, e.g. *'I've noticed that …', 'I've heard that …'*)?	
Have you punctuated sentences correctly with capital letters, full stops, commas, exclamation marks and question marks?	
Have you used the following correctly most of the time: speech marks, possessive apostrophes, dashes, colons, semicolons and parentheses?	
Have you used the correct spelling of common words?	
Have you used the correct spelling of unusual or difficult words?	
Have you provided an effective and convincing concluding statement that summarises your opinion, introduced by an appropriate phrase, e.g. *Consequently …, Admittedly …, In conclusion …, It's evident that …, Overall …, In considering these arguments …*?	

In this section we start with a sample of a narrative text. First we give some details about this type of writing, then there is a sample question with answers, and finally there are two practice Writing Tests for narrative texts.

Improving your narrative writing

For the Writing Test you might be asked to write a narrative. If you are, try to write in a way that is a true response and that indicates your interests.

Don't just write in a formal and rehearsed manner or by simply repeating something that is known to you. Look at the task and consider the following:

- Does it want me to set out a conversation?
- Does it want me to describe something?
- Does it want me to say how something happened?
- Does it want my point of view?
- Does it want me to write a poem?

When people are doing something that interests them, they achieve at a higher level. Try to include something that interests you in your writing.

Below are some ways to help you improve your writing and make it more interesting to read.

Tips for writing a narrative

- Always try to make the opening of a narrative interesting or exciting for the reader. Start with dialogue, suspenseful action or description.

  For example:

  "Where am I?" I yelled, to no one in particular, or *Smoke started eerily moving throughout the house, creeping under doors, choking me with every movement.*

- Take a look at the beginnings of some of your favourite books to see how the authors started their narratives.

- Try to make the characters in your narrative sound realistic and convincing. Give them appropriate names.

- Remember to describe what the characters look like and how they act and feel, using plenty of adjectives and adverbs.

  For example:

  relieved, grumpy, terrified, politely, mad, immature, fearlessly, angrily, daring, persuasive.

- Try to show their personalities in the things they do, say and think. Here are some examples:

  - *talkative*—someone who is friendly and chatty, someone who is inclined to talk a great deal, someone who is not quiet or shy or someone who might interrupt other people

  - *clumsy*—someone awkward, someone without skill or someone who is always breaking things

  - *confident*—someone sure of themselves or someone who is not shy or insecure.

  What type of character in your story (a talkative, clumsy or confident person) would be likely to say the following: *"I was sure I would be able to climb over the wall to escape"*?

- Build descriptions by using:

  - alliteration (words starting with the same letter).

    For example:

    the rising river rushed

  - rhyme.

    For example:

    hustle and bustle

- onomatopoeia (words that sound like the thing they describe).

  For example:

  crashed and banged

- similes and metaphors.

- Imagine that you are photographing everything you see happening.

- Expand sentences to explain who, what, how, where, when and why something happened.

  For example:

  The frightened boy collapsed wearily to the floor, then slowly grabbed the old, wrinkled and itchy blanket and pulled it over his shaking body.

- Write sentences of different lengths.

- Base your narrative on an unexpected chain of events, a catastrophe or a problem that needs to be solved. Narratives may even consist of more than one problem. They become exciting when things don't go as planned, when an accident has occurred or when someone or something gets lost or stolen. Suspense is also built up by slowly leading up to events. Instead of writing *The house collapsed*, use speech, description and action to build up to the event: *The wind was howling and the sound of thunder became louder and louder. We heard an almighty crash. "What was that?" I asked my brother Michael, with a shaky voice. "Just the wind," he replied, not too confidently. As bits of the ceiling crumbled all around us, I huddled up against Michael. "No, it's not just the wind," I replied, looking at the fearful look on his face. The house started to tremble and things were crashing and banging all around us. We ran, not looking behind us at all as the roof caved in and then everything went black.*

- Include dialogue between descriptions.

- Use questions.

- Start sentences in different ways.

- Think about the final sentence of your narrative. This is just as important as the opening sentence. Remember: this is the last thing that will be read, and this image is the one that will stay with the reader. The ending will need to explain how the problem was solved or the event resolved.

Alternative descriptive words

Make your writing more interesting by using alternatives for these common words.

BIG: large, huge, enormous, gigantic, vast, massive, colossal, immense, bulky, hefty, significant

GOT/GET: obtain, acquire, find, get hold of, gain, achieve, take, retrieve, reach, get back, recover, bring

WENT/GO: leave, reach, go away, depart, exit, move, quit, scramble, crawl, trudge, tread, trample, skip, march, shuffle, swagger, prance, stride, strut

GOOD: decent, enjoyable, superior, fine, excellent, pleasant, lovely, exquisite, brilliant, superb, tremendous

NICE: pleasant, good, kind, polite, fine, lovely

SAW/SEE: glimpse, notice, spot, witness, observe, watch, view, consider, regard, perceive, detect

SMALL: little, minute, short, tiny, miniature, petite, minor, unimportant, microscopic, minuscule, puny

HAPPY: content, pleased, glad, joyful, cheerful, in high spirits, ecstatic, delighted, cheery, jovial, satisfied, thrilled

SAD: depressed, gloomy, miserable, distressed, dismal, disappointed

BAD: awful, terrible, horrific, horrifying, horrendous, evil, naughty, serious, regretful, rotten, appalling, shocking, ghastly, dire, unpleasant, poor, frightening, inexcusable, atrocious, abysmal, sickening, gruesome, unspeakable, outrageous, disgusting, deplorable

GOING: leaving, departing, disappearing, separating, exiting

RUN: sprint, jog, scuttle, scamper, dart, dash, scurry, rush, hurry, trot

WALK: stroll, march, stride, pace, hike, stagger, move, wander, step, tread

SAID:					
	boasted	exclaimed	mumbled	replied	stammered
acknowledged	boomed	explained	murmured	requested	stated
added	bragged	expressed	nagged	responded	stormed
admitted	called	feared	noted	revealed	stuttered
advised	claimed	giggled	objected	roared	suggested
agreed	commanded	grinned	observed	screamed	taunted
alerted	commented	grunted	ordered	screeched	thought
announced	complained	indicated	pleaded	shouted	told
answered	cried	insisted	pointed out	shrieked	urged
argued	decided	instructed	questioned	snapped	uttered
asked	declared	laughed	rambled	sneered	wailed
babbled	demanded	lied	reassured	sobbed	warned
began	denied	mentioned	remarked	spoke	whined
blurted	emphasised	moaned	repeated	squealed	whispered

Useful adjectives

Using a variety of adjectives will add interest to your story.

A

able, absolute, active, adorable, adventurous, affectionate, alert, alive, almighty, amazing, amusing, ancient, angelic, angry, annoying, awful, awkward

B

babyish, bad, bald, bare, beautiful, bending, big, bitter, blunt, boastful, bold, boring, brainless, brainy, brave, brilliant, broken, brutal, busy

C

careful, caring, cautious, charming, chatty, childlike, chilly, chirpy, choosy, clean, clever, clumsy, cold, colourful, complete, confident, considerate, cool, correct, courageous, crazy, crooked, curious, cute

D

damaged, dangerous, daring, dazzling, deadly, delicate, delicious, desperate, determined, difficult, dirty, diseased, disgraceful, dishonest, disobedient, dreamy, dried, drowsy, dull, dusty

E

eager, easy, elderly, elegant, enchanting, energetic, enormous, entertaining, envious, excellent, exciting, experienced, expert, extreme

F

fabulous, faint, fair, faithful, false, fancy, fashionable, faultless, fearful, fearless, feeble, ferocious, fierce, fiery, fine, firm, fit, flabby, flashy, floppy, fluffy, foggy, foolish, forgetful, fortunate, fragrant, freaky, fresh, friendly, frightening, frightful, frosty, funny, fuzzy

G

generous, gentle, genuine, ghostly, gifted, glamorous, gloomy, glossy, good, gorgeous, graceful, great, greedy, grubby, grumpy

H

hairy, handsome, handy, happy, hard, harmless, hazy, healthy, heavenly, heavy, helpful, helpless, heroic, honest, hopeful, hopeless, horrible, horrific, hot, huge, humble, humorous, hungry, hurtful

I

icy, ignorant, immature, important, incredible, indescribable, inquisitive, invisible, irritable, itchy

J

jealous, jittery, joyful, juicy, jumpy

K

keen, kind

L

large, lazy, light, likeable, little, lively, loaded, lonely, long, loud, lousy, lovely, lucky, luxurious

M

mad, magical, magnificent, marvellous, massive, masterful, mature, mean, mighty, mindless, miniature, modern, modest, monstrous, muddy, musical, mysterious

N

nasty, natural, naughty, neat, nervous, new, nice, noisy, nosy, numb, nutritious, nutty

O

obedient, observant, occasional, odd, old, organised, original, outrageous, outstanding, overgrown

P

pale, paralysed, peaceful, peculiar, perfect, persistent, persuasive, picky, piercing, pimply, plain, playful, pleasant, pleasing, poisonous, polite, poor, popular, precious, pretty, priceless, prickly, proper, protective, proud, puffy, pushy, puzzling

Q

quarrelsome, queer, questionable, quick, quiet, quirky

R

radiant, rare, rattled, raw, reasonable, reckless, refreshing, relaxed, relieved, remarkable, respectable, restless, revolting, rich, rigid, rosy, rotten, round, rowdy, royal, rubbery, rude, rusty

S

sad, saggy, savage, scary, scheming, scrappy, scrawny, scruffy, scrumptious, secretive, selfish, sensible, serious, shaky, shapeless, shattered, shiny, shocking, short, shy, silent, sincere, skilful, skinny, sleek, sleepy, slimy, slippery, sloppy, slow, small, smart, smelly, smooth, snappy, sneaky, soapy, soft, solid, sorrowful, sour, sparkly, special, speedy, spellbound, spicy, spiky, spoilt, spooky, sporty, spotty, squeaky, stainless, sticky, stranded, strange, streaky, strong, stupid, stylish, sudden, sulky, sunny, super, sweet, swift

T

talkative, tall, tame, tearful, tedious, tempting, tender, terrible, terrifying, thirsty, thorny, thoughtful, thoughtless, thrilling, ticklish, tidy, timid, tiny, tiresome, traditional, trendy, tricky, troublesome, trusting, truthful, trying

U

ugly, unexpected, unfair, unfortunate, unkind, unknown, unsteady, unwell, unwilling

V

vain, valued, venomous, vicious, victorious, vigorous, violent, vulgar

W

wacky, warm, wasteful, weak, wealthy, weary, weird, well, wet, whimpering, wicked, wide, wiggly, wild, wise, wishful, witty, wobbly, wonderful, woolly, worthy, wrecked, wrinkly, wrongful

Y

young, youthful

Z

zany, zealous

Here is a Sample Writing question for a narrative text.

Topic: Invisible for a day

Today you are going to write a narrative or story. The idea for your story is **Invisible for a day**.

Imagine that you woke up one morning, put on your jumper and suddenly you were invisible.

Remember to:
- think about the characters
- make sure there is a complication or problem to be solved
- plan your writing
- use paragraphs
- write in sentences
- check your spelling and punctuation
- write at least one page.

SAMPLE ANSWERS: NARRATIVE WRITING

We have provided six sample answers to the sample question. We have grouped them into the three levels of ability used throughout this book. Please note that these are approximate guidelines only.

Invisible for a day

STANDARD LEVEL 1

i put on the jumper

i feld normal sally is sleep the windowe smasht

I got so scered i wont to go bak to sleep i tryed to tack of the jumper but it was stack

STANDARD LEVEL 2

Once upon a time I woke up and put on my jumper. I felt funny. I was scaird. It was strang. I worke around the house and went to the mirar to see how I lookd like I coodn't see me. I tatched my face I was ther but I thort wot is rong with you. I went to see my sista she was noormal then I thort a wich casted a spell on me then I woke to find it was all just a dream.

INTERMEDIATE LEVEL 1

So it was the first day of the holdays. I was so exited that I ran to put my cloths on and go outside to play with ben my frend. So I looked into the mirra and I wasn't there. This was cool. I could now do watever i wonted i mite go and play jocks on my sister or go wherevr i wonted grate!!! Hi everybody I yeld every one was scared. Its just me and every one was glad. I covered my self with my jumper so people could seem me then i went out to play with my frend BEN. The End.

INTERMEDIATE LEVEL 2

I woke up on the first day of the holidays. It was cold so I wore my jumper. my friend Ben was waiting for me at his house. I quickly looked into the mirror to see what I looked like and I wasn't there. This is cool! I can do what I want because I am invisible. I went to my sister and pulled her hair. She went ow! You can't see me. I went to mum and said hello. Where are you John she said? Here mum I said. But I can't see you mum said and started crying. I took my jumper off and then mum saw me. She was so happy. I won't go invisible again mum I said. After that she took me to Bens house so we can play.

Please note: Spelling, punctuation and grammar errors have been included to replicate the likely response of a Year 3 student.

ADVANCED LEVEL 1

Suddenly I was invisible and I also got the super power of being really fast. I felt dizzy. I began to spin so fast that I fell. I was scared and wanted to take off this jumper to get rid of the spell. I tried to take off the jumper but it was stack.

After telling my parents and friends what happened, I rode my bike to school where I acsidently knocked over a vase and the kids thort it was funny. My teacher saw it fall all by itself and thort she was going crazy! "This could be fun I said".

Later that day, I snucked down to parlamint and spied on the prime minster. Getting past sequrity was so easy. I took photos with my phone and sold them for a million dollars.

I told the news that I was invisible and i had super human speed. I became famous and got lots more money and I gave it to all my firends. Suddenly, I wasn't invisible anymore but I still had a million dollars so I lived happily ever after.

ADVANCED LEVEL 2

What a silly birthday present. I really wanted a soccer ball and all I get is this boring ugly red jumper. I thought I better put it on to make gran happy and so i did. I got up and went to get dressed. I went to the mirror to brush my hair, but I couldn't see my hair, I couldn't see my eyes, or even my nose. Was I invisible because of the jumper? Impossible! I started to wave at the mirror. Nothing!

This was not good. I was still in my little room, but what was happening to me? The itchy wool scratched my back and as I tried to pull off the jumper it got tighter and tighter! It was now 3 sizes too small and I let out a piercing cry, but gran couldn't hear me. The jumper got so tight that I couldn't even walk anymore! I was terrorfied and didn't know what to do. As I tried to take off the jumper suddenly it loosened by itself.

Then felt two strong hands grab me tightly. As I looked around I realised that I wasn't alone. The whole room was filled with invisible people wearing the same red coloured jumper. I was wondering what to do, when suddenly woke up to find it was all a dream, and a present with a big bow was sitting next to my bed. I hoped it wasn't a jumper!

Please note: Spelling, punctuation and grammar errors have been included to replicate the likely response of a Year 3 student.

WRITING TEST 3

In this part you will be doing some writing. Each Writing Test should take you 40 minutes. Write your answer on separate sheets of paper. Use the top part of the first sheet or the narrative text planning page to plan your ideas.

When you have finished, hand in your writing to your teacher, parents or another adult to mark it for you.

Topic: Three wishes

You find a bottle, you rub it and a genie will grant you three wishes. Describe what you would wish for and what it was like after the wishes came true.

Remember to:

- use paragraphs in your writing
- write in sentences
- check your spelling and punctuation
- write at least one page.

Here is a narrative text planning page to start you off. Use this page to plan your ideas.

NARRATIVE TEXT

INTRODUCTION/ORIENTATION: introduction of the main characters and setting

WHO?

WHAT?

WHEN?

WHERE?

COMPLICATION (PROBLEM): what triggered the problem
(There may be more than one.)

SEQUENCE OF EVENTS: what happens

BEGINNING

Connectives: *First(ly), next, later, after, afterwards, while, as, meanwhile, eventually, when, so, because, soon, consequently, immediately, previously, however, on the other hand, similarly, finally, despite this, otherwise ...*

MIDDLE

END

RESOLUTION: how the characters resolved the problem

CONCLUSION: the final outcome
Does it end with a question; a mystery; a statement; or with a coda (a moral or lesson learnt from the experience)?

Use this chart to evaluate your writing.

GUIDELINES FOR WRITING A NARRATIVE TEXT	✓ or ✗
Is there a clear beginning, middle and end?	
Is there a clear introduction stating who/what/where/when?	
Is the writing organised into paragraphs that focus on one idea?	
Does the writing develop a complication: create a problem, or trigger a surprising or unexpected chain of events?	
Have you added expression: feelings, thoughts, actions, what is seen, heard or felt?	
Have you used a variety of correct sentence structures including simple, compound and complex sentences?	
Have you used good adjectives/adverbs to build description and add information to your writing?	
Have you used imagery effectively, such as a simile or metaphor? e.g. *The sky lit up like fireworks* ...	
Have you used past/present/future tense accurately?	
Have you used pronouns correctly?	
Have you used verbs correctly: accurate tense and number, e.g. *he is*, *they are*?	
Have you used a variety of time connectives, e.g. *firstly*, *next*, *later*?	
Have you used a variety of conjunctions, e.g. *when*, *because*, *so*, *if*, *but*?	
Have you included dialogue?	
Have you punctuated sentences correctly with capital letters, full stops, commas, exclamation marks and question marks?	
Have you used the following correctly most of the time: speech marks, possessive apostrophes, dashes, colons, semicolons and parentheses?	
Have you used the correct spelling of common words?	
Have you used the correct spelling of unusual or difficult words?	
Does the writing end in an interesting way?	

In this part you will be doing some writing. Each Writing Test should take you 40 minutes. Write your answer on separate sheets of paper. Use the top part of the first sheet or the narrative text planning page to plan your ideas.

When you have finished, hand in your writing to your teacher, parents or another adult to mark it for you.

Topic: A day in the life of my pet

Imagine that you woke up and were transformed into your pet. Describe what pet you would be, what you would spend all day doing, and how you felt during this day.

Remember to:

- use paragraphs in your writing
- write in sentences
- check your spelling and punctuation
- write at least one page.

Use this narrative text planning page to plan your ideas.

NARRATIVE TEXT

INTRODUCTION/ORIENTATION: introduction of the main characters and setting

WHO?	WHAT?	WHEN?	WHERE?

COMPLICATION (PROBLEM): what triggered the problem
(There may be more than one.)

SEQUENCE OF EVENTS: what happens

BEGINNING

Connectives: *First(ly), next, later, after, afterwards, while, as, meanwhile, eventually, when, so, because, soon, consequently, immediately, previously, however, on the other hand, similarly, finally, despite this, otherwise ...*

MIDDLE

END

RESOLUTION: how the characters resolved the problem

CONCLUSION: the final outcome

Does it end with a question; a mystery; a statement; or with a coda (a moral or lesson learnt from the experience)?

CHECK YOUR SKILLS: WRITING TEST 4

Use this chart to evaluate your writing.

GUIDELINES FOR WRITING A NARRATIVE TEXT	✓ or ✗
Is there a clear beginning, middle and end?	
Is there a clear introduction stating who/what/where/when?	
Is the writing organised into paragraphs that focus on one idea?	
Does the writing develop a complication: create a problem, or trigger a surprising or unexpected chain of events?	
Have you added expression: feelings, thoughts, actions, what is seen, heard or felt?	
Have you used a variety of correct sentence structures including simple, compound and complex sentences?	
Have you used good adjectives/adverbs to build description and add information to your writing?	
Have you used imagery effectively, such as a simile or metaphor? e.g. *The sky lit up like fireworks* ...	
Have you used past/present/future tense accurately?	
Have you used pronouns correctly?	
Have you used verbs correctly: accurate tense and number, e.g. *he is*, *they are*?	
Have you used a variety of time connectives, e.g. *firstly*, *next*, *later*?	
Have you used a variety of conjunctions, e.g. *when, because, so, if, but*?	
Have you included dialogue?	
Have you punctuated sentences correctly with capital letters, full stops, commas, exclamation marks and question marks?	
Have you used the following correctly most of the time: speech marks, possessive apostrophes, dashes, colons, semicolons and parentheses?	
Have you used the correct spelling of common words?	
Have you used the correct spelling of unusual or difficult words?	
Does the writing end in an interesting way?	

GLOSSARY OF GRAMMAR AND PUNCTUATION TERMS

Adjectival clause

An adjectival clause provides further information about the person or thing named. It functions as an adjective, describing a noun and answering the questions What? Who? How many? or Which?

This is the bike that was given to me by Dad.

An adjectival clause contains a subject and verb and usually begins with a relative pronoun (*who*, *whom*, *whose*, *which* or *that*).

Adjectival phrase

An adjectival phrase is a group of words, usually beginning with a preposition or a participle, that acts as an adjective, giving more information about a noun.

The man in the blue jumper is my uncle. (preposition)

The man wearing the blue jumper is my uncle. (participle)

Adjective

An adjective is a word used to describe and give more information about a noun.

Some examples include *multiple books, a delicious cake, my gorgeous friend.*

Adverb

An adverb is a word used to describe or give more information about a verb, an adjective or another adverb, to tell us how, when or where the action happened. Adverbs often end in *-ly*.

The flag flapped wildly in the wind. (how)

I always brush my teeth in the morning. (when)

He slid downwards towards the side of the boat. (where)

Adverbial clause

An adverbial clause acts like an adverb. It functions as an adverb, giving more information about the verb, usually telling when, where or how. It indicates manner, place or time, condition, reason, purpose or result.

Water is important because plant and animal communities depend on water for food, water and shelter. (reason)

Adverbial phrase

An adverbial phrase is a group of words, usually beginning with a preposition, that acts as an adverb, giving more information about the time, manner or place of the verb, telling us where, when, how far, how long, with what, with whom, and about what.

Chloe hit Ava with the old broom.

Apostrophe

An apostrophe is a form of punctuation used to show:

1. a contraction (missing letters in a word), e.g. *can't = cannot*
2. possession, e.g. *David's book, the boys'* (plural) *mother*

Brackets ( )

Brackets are a form of punctuation used to include an explanatory word, phrase or sentence.

He took the book from his friend (Anthony) but never returned it.

Capital letter

Capital letters are used at the beginning of sentences, as well as for proper nouns, e.g. the names of people, places, titles, countries and days of the week.

Colon (:)

A colon is a form of punctuation used to introduce information, such as a list, or further information to explain the sentence.

GLOSSARY OF GRAMMAR AND PUNCTUATION TERMS

The following should be taken on the trip: a warm jacket, socks, jeans, shirts and shoes.

The warning read: "Give up now or else!"

Comma (,)

A comma is a form of punctuation used to break up the parts of a sentence, or to separate words or phrases in a list.

The children, who have not completed their homework, will be punished.

My brother likes to eat peanuts, steaks, oranges and cherries.

Conjunction/connective

A conjunction or connective is a word joining parts of a sentence or whole sentences.

Conjunctions: *and, but, where, wherever, after, since, whenever, before, while, until, as, by, like, as if, though, because, so that, in order to, if, unless, in case, although, despite, whereas, even though*

My button fell off because it was not sewn on properly.

Connectives: *in other words, for example, therefore, then, next, previously, finally, firstly, to conclude, in that case, however, despite this, otherwise*

First we do our homework, and then we go out to play.

Dash (—)

A dash is a form of punctuation used to indicate a break or pause in a sentence.

Life is like giving a concert while you are learning to play the instrument—now that is really living.

We really hoped that he would stay—maybe next time.

Exclamation mark (!)

An exclamation mark is a form of punctuation used to mark the end of a sentence where strong emotions or reactions are expressed.

Ouch! I cut my finger.

I listened at the door. Nothing!

Full stop (.)

A full stop is a form of punctuation used to indicate the end of a sentence. Full stops are used before the closing of quotation marks.

David sat under the tree.

Nicholas said, "Come with me, James."

Imagery

Imagery includes:

Metaphor is when one thing is compared to another by referring to it as *being* something else, e.g. *The thief looked at her with a vulture's eye.*

Simile is comparing two different things using the words *as* or *like*, e.g. *The hail pelted down like bullets. He was as brave as a lion.*

Personification is giving human qualities or characteristics to non-human things, e.g. *Trees were dancing in the wind.*

Alliteration is the repetition of consonant sounds at the beginning of successive words for effect, e.g. *The sun sizzled softly on the sand. The rising river rushed.*

Onomatopoeia is the formation of words to imitate the sound a certain thing or action might make, e.g. *banged, crashed, hissed, sizzled.*

Repetition is repeating words or phrases for effect, e.g. *Indeed there will be time, time to relax, time to enjoy the sun and surf, time to be oneself once more.*

GLOSSARY OF GRAMMAR AND PUNCTUATION TERMS

Modality

Modality is the range of words used to express different degrees of probability, inclination or obligation. Modality can be expressed in a number of ways:

- Verbs: *can, could, should, might, must, will, it seems, it appears*
- Adverbs: *perhaps, possibly, generally, presumably, apparently, sometimes, always, never, undoubtedly, certainly, absolutely, definitely*
- Nouns: *possibility, opportunity, necessity*
- Adjectives: *possible, promising, expected, likely, probable.*

Noun

Nouns are words used to represent a person, place or thing. There are different types of nouns:

Common nouns are nouns that represent things in general, e.g. *boy, desk, bike.*

Proper nouns take a capital letter. They represent a particular thing, rather than just a general thing. Proper nouns are used to name a place, person, title, day of the week, month and city/country, e.g. *Michaela, November, Monday, Madagascar.*

Abstract nouns are things we cannot see but can often feel, e.g. *sadness, honesty, pride, love, hate, issue, advantages.*

Collective nouns are nouns that name a group of things, e.g. *herd, litter, team, flock.*

Preposition

Prepositions are words that connect a noun or pronoun to another word in the sentence. They also indicate time, space, manner or circumstance.

I am sitting between my brother and sister.

Some common prepositions are *in, at, on, to, by, into, onto, inside, out, under, below, before, after, from, since, during, until, after, off, above, over, across, among, around, beside, between, down, past, near, through, without.*

Pronoun

A pronoun is a word that is used in place of a noun. Pronouns refer to something that has already been named, e.g. *My brother is 10 years old. He is taller than me.*

Be careful of repetition and ambiguous use of pronouns: <u>He</u> went to the shops with <u>his friend</u> and <u>he</u> told <u>him</u> to wait outside.

The pronouns are *I, you, me, he, she, it, we, they, mine, yours, his, hers, ours, theirs, myself, ourselves, herself, himself, themselves, yourself, this, that, these, those, each, any, some, all, one, who, which, what, whose, whom.*

Question mark (?)

Question marks are needed at the end of any sentence that asks something, e.g. *What did you say?*

If a question is asked in an indirect way it does not have a question mark, e.g. *I asked him what he said.*

Quotation marks (" ")

Quotation marks have several uses.

- They are used to show the exact words of the speaker:

  John said, "I prefer the colour blue."

  "What are you doing?" asked Marie.

  "I like cats," said Sophia, "but I like dogs too."

When there is more than one speaker, a new line should be used when the new person begins to speak:

"What should we do now?" asked Ellen.

"I'm not too sure," whispered Jonathan.

- They are used when writing the names of books and movies.
- They are used when quoting exact words or phrases from a text.

Semicolon (;)

A semicolon is a form of punctuation used to separate clauses. It is stronger than a comma but not as final as a full stop.

Eighteen people started on the team; only twelve remain.

In our class we have people from Melbourne, Victoria; Sydney, New South Wales; and Brisbane, Queensland.

Sentence

A sentence is a group of words consisting of one or more clauses. It will begin with a capital letter and end with a full stop, question mark or exclamation mark.

Simple sentence: *I caught the bus.*

Compound sentence: *I caught the bus and arrived at school on time.*

Complex sentence: *Since I managed to get up early, I caught the bus.*

Tense

Tense is the form of the verb (a doing word) that tells us when something is happening in time—present, past or future.

I look, I am looking (present)

I will look (future)

I looked, I was looking (past)

Auxiliary verbs (e.g. *be*, *have* and *do*) help change the verb to express time, e.g. *I have looked, I have been looking, I had looked, I had been looking, I will have looked, I will have been looking.*

Verb

A verb is a word that expresses an action, e.g. I *ran*, he *forgot*, she *went*, Mary *shouted*. It can also express a state, e.g. *the boys are laughing*, *he is clever*, *he was all smiles*, *I know my spelling words*.

Active verb: The verb is in the active voice when the subject of the sentence does the action, e.g. <u>James</u> *broke the glass*. (*James* is the subject of this sentence.)

Passive verb: The passive voice tells you what happens to or what is being done to the subject, e.g. *The glass was broken by James.* (Here *the glass* is the subject of the sentence.)

The passive is often used in informative writing, where it is not always necessary to state the doer of an action, or the doer is not known, or it is not relevant.

Congratulations!

You have now finished all of the practice tests. This was a considerable effort and you deserve a reward for all this hard work! We hope that these tests were of some help to you. We wish you every success in your schooling.

Reader comments

Thank you for using this guide to the NAPLAN Tests. We hope that you found the practice tests helpful for your students or your child. If you have any comments or questions, we would be pleased to respond. Also let us know if you found any errors or omissions. We benefit from this feedback as it often highlights matters we have overlooked.

NUMERACY TEST 1 (pp. 22–28)

1. **6 TENS 7 ONES**. There are 67 ✳ shapes.

2. The largest number is **963**. Remember that if you want to change your answer just erase it and colour in the circle you want.

3. The **second piece of wood** is the longest. Did you pick this easily?

4. The cylinder is the **first object**.

5. The **first answer** is correct. We have tried to show this below (it is not drawn to scale). When you put both halves together then you would get a pentagon.

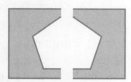

6. **$3.80**. The coins are
$2 + 10c + 50c + 20c + $1 = $3.80.

7. **7**. There are 28 crayons and each child is given four crayons. So there must be seven children (7 × 4 = 28 or 28 ÷ 4 = 7).

8. **Germany**. France is first, then Austria and Germany is third on 7 points.

9. The **second answer** is correct. It is the largest angle. The space between the lines is widest. Don't let the length of the lines confuse you. It is the size of the opening that is important.

10. ⊙ is at B2. Remember to count across the bottom first, then count upwards.

11. **5 × 4 = 20**. There are four wheels on each car. There are five cars, so the sum is 5 × 4 = 20. Did you write your answers in the spaces?

12. **The match is on 15 July**. To find the answer just work backwards: 18 Thursday, 17 Wednesday, 16 Tuesday, 15 Monday.

13. 🕗 is 8:00 (**second picture**).

14. **8**. There are 32 squares and each picture covers four squares.

15. **3 weeks**

16. ☺. The symbol ☺ looks the same when it is turned over horizontally. This is what we mean by *flipped*.

17. **39 cm**. The first rope is 78 cm and this is 39 cm more than the second rope.
It is 78 − 39 = 39.

18. **2 triangles** should be coloured. There are eight triangles and one-quarter would be any two of the triangles.

19. **230**. The numbers increase by 100. We start with 30 then add 100 to make 130. Then we add 100 to 130 to make 230. Did you write your answer in the rectangle?

20. ✋. The pattern is: there are two ✋ then two ✌ then two ☝ and finally two 👌. After the last 👌 then comes the ✋ symbol.

21. **25**. There were 9 Magpies and 16 Pigeons (9 + 16 = 25).

22. **B**. This is H-shaped with five blocks. The others are quite different.

23. **$10.50**. Each football costs $3.50 so three footballs will be three times $3.50.

24. **My book and phone together are the same length as my computer.** The computer is 30 cm; the book is 20 cm and the phone is 10 cm, so 20 cm + 10 cm = 30 cm. Do you understand how to read the chart?

25. **5**. Gordon answered five questions correctly.

26. **Patterson**. Patterson answered 10 questions correctly and this was the largest number.

27. **1 out of 6 chances**. When you spin the arrow it could land anywhere. There are six sections so the chance of landing in one of them is called one-in-six. It is the same when you throw a dice. Sometimes it will be a five and sometimes it will not. Overall we expect that it will be the number that we want about one in every six times.

28. **A**. This has only one out of the four spaces coloured.

29. **6**. There are six triangular prisms. The diagram below shows the triangular prisms.

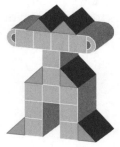

30. Fred 12 dollars and Jenny 6 dollars. This is because $18 = 12 + 6$ and one had to be twice as much as the other.

31. The **house** is always on the right-hand side. It is NEVER on the left. Did you notice that the word NEVER was in capital letters? This gives you a hint.

32. 170. The true answer to the sum is $30 + 61 + 80$ which is 171 and the closest number is 170. A little tricky, don't you think? Be careful and try to draw the problem on a sheet of paper.

33. 11 dots. The series is 1, 3, 5, 7, 9 and 11. Can you see the sequence? Add 2 to each number to get the next in the sequence.

34. B. This pathway is $20 + 35 + 20 + 25 = 100$.

35. $\frac{1}{2}$. A half of a half is a quarter.

36. A = 8 B = 12 If you insert the numbers in the puzzle and follow the arrows then this should make sense. The other answers are not correct.

NUMERACY TEST 2 (pp. 31–38)

1. 49. There are 49 sticks. There are four bundles of ten (40) and nine single sticks (9).

2. $\frac{1}{2}$. One half of the shape is coloured.
Remember that if you want to change your answer just erase it and colour in the circle you want.

3. It is more than 10. There are millions of stars in the sky. On a clear night you can probably see many hundreds even without a telescope. Did you pick this easily? (Note that the types of questions are changing in this test. Some will be the same but there will also be some new ones for you.)

4. The answer is the **5c + 10c + 20c (first box)**. This gives you 35 cents.

5. The **first** answer is correct. We have tried to show this below (it is not drawn to scale). When you put both halves together then you would get a cross.

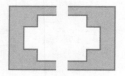

6. $5 + 9 = 14$. There are 14 crayons altogether. There are five in one group and nine in the other.

7. 15 June. Just take one week or seven days from 22 June.

8. 12. Red scored 15 and Yellow scored 3 so the difference is 12. There are two steps in this problem. First you have to find the teams and their scores. Then in the second step you have to subtract the points.

9. The **second answer** is correct. It is the largest angle. The space between the lines is widest. Don't let the length of the lines confuse you. It is the size of the opening that is important.

10. How Do You Do Town is in D2. Remember to count across the bottom first then count upwards.

11. 60 ÷ 10 = 6. The wood is 60 centimetres in length. Each piece will be 10 cm, so the calculation is $60 ÷ 10 = 6$. Did you write your answers in the boxes?

12. 9 + 9 + 9. You can divide the shape into smaller sections. There are three sections, or slices, of the shape with 9 cubes.

13. ✹ is 10:00 am (**second clock**). The time is ten o'clock in the morning. The other clocks show 4 am, 8 am or 9 am. All of these are earlier than 10 am.

14. 12. Twelve hexagons are needed. There are four rows and three columns.

15. They are all squares.

16. W. The letter W looks the same when it is turned over horizontally. This is what we mean by *flipped*.

17. 22. Bob has drawn 82 and Ian has drawn 60. It is $82 - 60 = 22$.

18. 2 shapes should be coloured. There are six shapes and one-third would be any two of the six shapes.

19. 150. The numbers increase by 100. We start with 50 then add 100 to make 150. Then we add 100 to 150 to make 250. Did you write your answer in the rectangle?

20. ⋀. There are four stars ⋀ ✦ ★ ✸; they start with a three-pointed star then a four-pointed then five-pointed and then six-pointed star. Did you see the pattern or did you find it hard to see that they increased? In this case it was the turn of the three-pointed star to come next. We hope this wasn't too tricky for you.

21. **Monaco**. Monaco has a coastline of only 4 km. It is a small country on the Mediterranean Sea on the south of France.

22. **40 minutes**. One kilometre takes 10 minutes so 4 kilometres will take 40 minutes (10 + 10 + 10 + 10 = 40).

23. **B**. The others are quite different.

24. **Flip**. The coloured shape has been flipped over.

25. **Hobart**. Hobart is the coldest city. The temperature is now 13 degrees Celsius. Did you know that the temperature is measured in degrees and that °C means degrees Celsius? This is the way we measure temperature.

26. **The temperature in Adelaide is now more than the forecast high for the day**. This must seem a little strange at first. You might be asking yourself how can the temperature now be lower than the high? This is because the high temperature is what the weather bureau *thinks* the temperature will be. It can change. We hope this wasn't too tricky for you. Ask someone to explain this if it isn't clear to you.

27. **Karttika**. The month of Karttika starts on 23 October and goes for 30 days. So 26 October is in that month.

28. **60**. The answer to this sum is 59 so 60 is the closest estimate. To estimate it we changed the sum to 30 + 30 = 60.

29. **Top**. It is 1 out of 2 chances for the top row. The middle row is 1 out of 3 chances and the bottom row is 1 out of 4 chances. 1 out of 4 is worse than 1 out of 3 and both are worse than 1 out of 2. You have the best chance of picking the glasses or spectacles in the top row.

30. **A**. This has only 4 out of the 16 spaces coloured. Four is one quarter of 16. Don't worry if you didn't know that 4 is a quarter of 16.

31. **18**. The multiples are 10, 15, 20, 25, 30, 35, 40, 45, 50, 55, 60, 65, 70, 75, 80, 85, 90, 95.

32. **Any number from 1 to 6 is possible**. When you throw the dice it is certain the number will be from 1 to 6. All numbers have the same chance.

33. The correct answer is shown here. The big trick is to find the 1 or the 2 first then the other numbers are easy.

34. **A**. This pathway is 8 + 32 + 38 + 22 = 100.

35. **6**. We start with 8 then add 7 to give 15. Three get off so that leaves 15 − 3 = 12. Half get off and a half of 12 is 6 so that leaves 12 − 6 = 6 children still on the bus.

36. **8**. If you double 8 you get 16 and if you then add 8 this gives you 24.

NUMERACY TEST 3 (pp. 40–46)

1. **472**. There are 4 hundreds, 7 tens and 2 units. This question was a little different than before. Were you able to understand what had to be done?

2. **7**. There were seven birthdays in August because there were seven candles. Remember that if you want to change your answer just erase it and colour in the circle you want.

3. **Circle, triangle, rectangle**. There is one circle, three rectangles and two triangles in the picture. Note that the types of questions are also changing in this test. Some will be the same but there will also be some new ones for you.

4. The answer is the **first group** of coins **$1 + 50c + 20c + 5c**. This gives you $1.75.

5. The **first answer** is correct. We have tried to show this below (it is not drawn to scale). When you put both halves together then you would get a diamond.

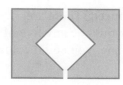

6. **6 + 6 + 6 + 6 + 6 + 6 + 6 = 42**. There are 42 pieces of fruit altogether. There are six in one group and there are seven trees.

7. **2**. There are 20 hats. So there must be 6 hats in each group (6 × 3 = 18 or 6 + 6 + 6 = 18) and this leaves two left over.

8. **Lungs** are the third heaviest at 600 grams.

9. The **first answer** is the right angle. It is shown below.

10. **Garden Street then Holmes Street**. You pass along Garden Street then Holmes Street to get to Anzac Parade.

11. **West**. Anzac Parade is to the west of Edgar Street.

12. **60 ÷ 5= 12**. The wood is 60 centimetres in length. Each piece will be 5 cm, so the calculation is 60 ÷ **5 = 12**. Did you write your answers in the boxes?

13. is closest to 7:30 (**second clock**).

14. **15 metres**. The edges were at 25 metres and 40 metres on the tape, so the distance is 15 metres.

15. **They are all ellipses**. An ellipse looks like an egg on its side.

Each of the ellipses overlaps and might be hard for you to see.

16. **H**. The letter H looks the same when it is turned over horizontally. This is what we mean by *flipped*.

17. **4**. There are 24 flowers. You can make four bunches with six roses in each

18. **5 shapes should be coloured**. There are 10 shapes and one-half would be any five of the ten shapes. For example, you could colour just the top half.

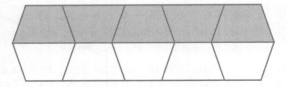

19. **86**. The numbers decrease by 7. We start with 100 then subtract to make 93. Then we subtract another 7 from 93 to make 86. Did you write your answer in the rectangle?

20. 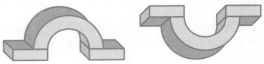. The pattern is: there are three objects followed by a new set of three. The flower would have been the second in the set. We hope this wasn't too tricky for you.

21. **TV**. The light bulb is lowest with 100 watts and the TV is second lowest with 250 watts.

22. **3**. The $10 note is twice as much as the $5 note: the $20 note is twice as much as the $10 note; the $100 note is twice as much as the $50 note.

23. **C**. The others are slightly different. Here is the original and the copy. The copy is turned over.

24. **Turn**. The shape has been turned or rotated.

25. **Gulf War**. The Gulf War was the shortest war. It lasted for one year (1991).

26. **The war in Afghanistan is longer than World War 2**. We hope this wasn't too tricky for you. Ask someone to explain this if it isn't clear to you.

27. **multiply $10 000 by five**. The largest book in the world is a photography book. It is called *Bhutan: A Visual Odyssey* and it is about 2 metres by 1½ metres in size. To order five copies you need to multiply the price by five so you would need $50 000 to buy this book for your five friends!

28. **130 cm**. The answer to the sum is 127 because 41 + 29 + 38 + 19 = 127 and 130 is the closest number. To estimate it you could have changed the sum to 40 + 30 + 40 + 20 = 130.

29. **An odd number is an even number plus one**.

30. **8 × (6 + 4) = 80**. First you add 6 and 4 to give 10 then you multiply by 8 to give 80.

31. **The answer to the addition is always a multiple of three**. You can check this: 1 + 2 + 3 = 6; or 2 + 3 + 4 = 9; or 3 + 4 + 5 = 12; or 4 + 5 + 6 = 15 and so on. All the answers are multiples of three. Do you know why?

32. **6**. The different ways of scoring a seven are: 1 + 6; 2 + 5; 3 + 4 and 6 + 1; 5 + 2; 4 + 3. You might only have listed three ways.

33. The correct answer is shown here. The big trick is to find the 12 or the 13 first then the other numbers are easy. Remember that all three sides need to equal 44.

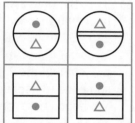

34. **A**. This pathway is $200 - 120$ which gives 80; then $80 \div 2 = 40$; then $40 + 60$ equals 100.

35. **B**. Here is the complete pattern.

Notice that there are semicircles across the top row and only rectangles in the bottom row. Next, the first column has one line in the middle but the second column has two lines in the middle. Thirdly, the pattern of the orange circle and the triangle change from the first column to the second column. There are three things happening at once. Don't worry if this was hard for you. It wasn't an easy question.

36. **35**. These numbers are all spaced 7 apart: 14, 21, 28, 35, 42.

NUMERACY TEST 4 (pp. 48–55)

1. **The third answer is correct**. The other numbers are smaller (472, 274, and 473). Were you able to understand what had to be done?

2. **934**. Remember: if you want to change your answer just erase it and colour in the circle you want.

3. **3**. $9 - 6 = 3$

4. **11**. $8 + 3 = 11$.

5. **12**. $6 \times 2 = 12$.

6. **cross**. There is one round smiley face, one cross and one heart. This should have been fairly easy for you.

7. The answer is the **first group** of notes: $\$5 + \$10 + \$20 + \$50 = \$85$.
(Note that the types of questions are also changing in this test. Some will be the same but there will also be some new ones for you.)

8. **1 and 4**. We have tried to show this below (it is not drawn to scale). When you put both halves together then you would get a diamond.

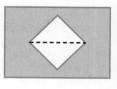

9. **$4 \times 5 = 20$**. There are 20 roofs altogether. There are four temples with five roofs each.

10. **6**. There are 20 numbers. So there must be 7 numbers in each group ($7 \times 2 = 14$) and this leaves six left over.

11. **Rock around the clock**. This is the third most popular song and the third highest in sales.

12. **The left side is heavier than the right**. The left side on the scale or balance (as you look at it) is heavier because it is lower down.

13. **Megisti**. This is closest to D3.

14. **Megisti to Ai lias**. This is a map of a small island in Greece. Did the strange names make it difficult for you?

15. **A and C**. The correct pieces are shown below. Did you write your answers in the boxes?

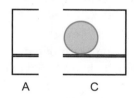

16. **60 minutes**. It is now 9:30 and in one hour or 60 minutes it will be 10:30.

17. **16** squares (grey and white) are needed to cover the space. This is shown in the picture below.

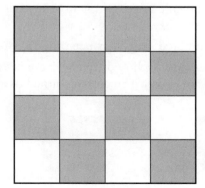

18. **It is a diamond**. If you connect all the diamonds with a line, you will have drawn a diamond.

19. **4 centimetres**. The face is about twice as wide as the mouth.

20. The shapes are grouped by number. There are five shapes in each group.

21. **78**.

22. **8**.

23. **$185**. The sum is:
$5 + $10 + $20 + $50 + $100 = $185.

24. The pattern starts with 2 o'clock, then 4 o'clock then 6 o'clock, then 8 o'clock and finally 10 o'clock. These are all even numbers.

25. **D**. This shape has four triangles coloured. The pattern is one triangle coloured then two triangles coloured, then three triangles coloured and finally four triangles coloured.

26. **13**. The numbers decrease by 13. We start with 65 then subtract 13 to make 52. Then we subtract another 13 from 52 to make 39. Was this a little hard for you? If so, don't worry as we are trying to make the questions in this test a little more challenging. Did you write your answers in the boxes?

27. **Flip**. The coloured shape has been flipped over.

28. **A**. The others are slightly different. Here is the original and the copy. The copy is turned over.

29. **Pharos of Alexandria**. This was a great lighthouse that was built in 279 BC. It was 124 m high and it was the tallest lighthouse ever built. It took 20 years to build but it was destroyed by an earthquake in 1375. You may not know about the Seven Wonders of the Ancient World but this table gives you some of the facts. Remember: years that are BC (Before Christ) go backwards in time. Don't worry if you have not learnt about BC dates.

30. **The distance around the pyramid is just over 900 metres**. This distance is 230 + 230 + 230 + 230 = 920. You don't have to calculate it exactly. You have to add the 230 metres on each side. Ask someone to explain this if it isn't clear to you. We hope this wasn't too tricky for you.

31. **Multiply 724 by five**. To estimate or guess how many televisions are owned you need to multiply the estimated number (724) by five so there would be 3620 televisions for 5000 people!

32. **The square with the seven dots was missing**. The squares increase from 1, 3, 5, 7 and then 9. These are all odd numbers.

33. ÷ **and** −. It is the division then the minus sign. The sum is $20 \div (10 - 5) = 4$. If you don't know how to do this, ask for some help.

34. **2**. The ballpoint pen was developed in 1938 and sliced bread was developed in 1928.

35. **24**. If you subtract 1904 from 1928 then the answer is 24.

36. ✶✶✦. Two asterisks (six-pointed star) equal one circle. One four-pointed star is equal to one circle. Two circles equal one square. Therefore one square equals two asterisks and one star. This is quite complicated. Don't worry if it's a little strange to you at first. We have tried to show this in a different way below:

✶✶ = ○
✦ = ○
□ = ○○

Therefore
□ = ✶✶✦

READING TEST 1 (pp. 57–63)

1. **The rabbit is looking at a sign**. The rabbit cannot read (although it might seem that it can read from the drawing). It is not a street sign and the sign does not give directions to rabbits.

2. *Solomon Grundy* **is a poem.**

3. **Solomon Grundy**

4. **Wednesday**. Solomon Grundy was married on Wednesday.

5. **children.** *Solomon Grundy* is a popular poem that was written for children in England. It is a type of nursery rhyme.

6. **It is a fairy tale about a man and a boy**. This is the cover from the book *Pinocchio*, which is a well-known fairy tale about a man and the puppet that he made. Perhaps you have read it. If not, why not try to read it and see if it interests you?

7. Channel Seven ends at **1.30 am**.

8. This program guide is for **Sunday**. You can see this from the programs Soccer Sunday, Sunday Sunrise and others.

9. There are **5** sporting programs on Channel Two — Soccer Sunday, Cricket, Tenpin Bowling, Soccer: European Champions League and Tennis Highlights.

10. **Lisa Murray**, **Henry Curley** and **Miles Tipota**. Any one of these would be correct.

11. **Worldwatch**, **News and Weather**, **Latenight News**. Any one of these would be correct.

12. *rpt* means that the program is a **repeat**. It has been shown before.

13. **Letter to a Wizard**

14. **black pointy hat** and a **cloak**.

15. This poem is about **wanting to be a wizard**.

16. **She thinks it would be fun**.
    She would like to fly a broomstick.
    She would like to create spells.

17. **in a book**

18. **to teach us to help the poor**

19. **coins**

20. **We should help the poor because one day we might also need help.**

21. **B.** Did you colour in one circle? This picture shows a boy leaving his work to chase after a mouse. It is something he is unlikely to catch. The saying teaches us that we should hold on to what we have and not chase after things we might never gain.

22. **A.** This picture shows some boys stranded by the tide. It teaches us that the world and time are passing and that things in life will not wait—life goes on. You should make use of the time you have and the chances you are given.

23. **D.** This picture shows a girl who is sad because she has broken a jug and spilt some milk. However, the cats are happy because they get to drink some nice milk. The saying shows that even when something goes wrong in life there will always be someone who gains.

24. **Blue (da ba dee)**. This is the full name of the song.

25. **It is a song about a little man that lives in a blue world**.

26. **Everything he sees is blue**.

27. h**is house, the window, a Corvette**

28. **because there is no-one to talk to**. He does not have anyone to listen to him.

29. **Hi**. There are many different meanings of the word *Yo* but the only answer that makes sense in this song is *Hi*.

30. **776 BC**

31. **Zeus**. Zeus is the only name of a god.

32. **Athens**

33. **were held every four years; invited all Greek citizens to compete.**

34. **The purpose of the text is to inform**.

35. **It begins the story of the Olympics**.

36. **All Greeks were invited to attend and participate**. This is incorrect, as women were not permitted to attend the first Olympics.

37. The word *sacrifice* means **offering**.

38. To begin with, the festival lasted for **1 day**.

39. A *diaulus* is **a type of race**. It is a foot race.

ANSWERS TO READING TESTS

READING TEST 2 (pp. 65–72)

1. **It is a fairy tale about a man and little people.**
2. **The rabbit is doing arithmetic.**
3. **The rabbit in this drawing cannot be real.**
4. **He stepped in a puddle of water.**
5. **Gloucester.** This is a tricky question.
6. **The barbecue is on Sunday.**
7. **No**
8. **Jason asked Pece to his birthday party.**
9. **He eats hamburgers; he goes to discos; he is popular; he plays Aussie Rules.**
10. **He is a 'Maco' kid; He is new; He is religious; He learns dancing; He likes savoury pastries; He plays soccer.**
11. **Yes**
12. **Yes**
13. **Pete**
14. **a reflection of the dog**
15. **It tried to get another bone.**
16. **greedy**
17. **The dog tricked itself.**
18. **The dog lost the bone.**
19. **It teaches us that greedy people can lose everything.**
20. **child**
21. **The family is on vacation near the sea.**
22. **The mother is happy because she is free from her everyday jobs.**
23. **The father is happy because he has two weeks' holiday.**
24. **Christmas Vacation** would be a good name for the poem.
25. **for fame and fortune**
26. **New York is fast, big and exciting.**
27. **fast.** *Fast* is an adjective or describing word. *Fame* and *fortune* are the names of things and are both nouns.
28. **A Gift from France** would be a good title.
29. **something you buy**
30. The gift came from **France**.
31. *Clutch* means **hold tightly**.
32. **Peek** means the same as *glimpse*.
33. **214**
34. **trouble breathing, heavy sweating, stomach pain**
35. The correct thing to do would be to **bandage up the area tightly and don't move the victim at all**. If you are not certain which answer to choose then eliminate those that you are sure are wrong. Then make a guess from those that are left over.
36. **immediately**
37. **stop, help**. Did you pay attention to the word BOTH?
38. **Putting pressure on the bite will stop the venom spreading**. Some of the other answers are almost correct (for example, the funnel-web has a large body of 3 cm, without the legs).
39. **violent**

READING TEST 3 (pp. 74–80)

1. Brite! is prepared in **Australia**. Careful: the question asks for a country, not a city.
2. **The label informs customers as to what is in the bottle or can.**
3. **Purchaser** is similar in meaning to *consumer*.
4. **654**
5. **It is a book of wonderful tales of the Arab world.**
6. **sultans, princes, camels, oases**
7. **an invitation**
8. **Greenplace Primary School**
9. The fete will be open from **10 am to 4 pm**.
10. **all of the above**
11. **She is following the footprints of the dog.**
12. **This dog is smarter than the girl.**
13. **Little Bird in the Tree**
14. **the bird**

15. cares

16. when there are two Michaels in a school

17. He is tall and dark-haired.

18. People feel curious when they meet someone with the same name.

19. It is a mix-up.

20. when the letter is addressed to M Smith

21. **Bianca.** Bianca meets someone with the same name and wonders what the other person is like.

22. Ask Mum or Dad to help.

23. polyester

24. 20 seconds

25. children over 8 years with adult help

26. A bogy is not a real thing.

27. Adults were afraid of bogies.

28. It came from the British Isles.

29. the bogies that were on roads on dark nights

30. to make children behave

31. **lurked.** *Lurked* means 'hanging around and waiting'.

32. Slang is the special sayings that a certain group of people use.

33. After some hard yakka in the garden, the workers have a smoko.

34. *Australian-made* is about the colourful language that has been developed in this country.

35. Australians are famous for their use of colourful language.

36. for about 200 years

37. hot

38. The first sentence tells the reader what each paragraph is about.

39. Newcomers may never have heard our slang.

READING TEST 4 (pp. 82–89)

1. It is about other countries and their people.

2. The man is taking two tyres from someone else's car.

3. He looks astonished.

4. Jan Weeks

5. There was a hole in Santa's pants.

6. It happened a week before Christmas.

7. It was at the North Pole; the air was cold; there was snow.

8. He was angry because he was loud and cross.

9. a man

10. How To Do Magic Tricks.

11. preparation

12. 3

13. It means having everything ready.

14. **patter.** Patter is the small talk or conversation that a magician makes to distract the audience.

15. Belt; jacket; pockets where you can hide things; shirt with long sleeves, pockets and buttons; trousers.

16. **Healthy food makes you stronger.** This is shown in the title.

17. fresh fruit

18. bread, rice and pasta

19. once every now and then

20. eating

21. 13 000

22. 6000

23. rice, fish

24. It is the fifth largest country in the world.

25. Indonesia is between the Indian and Pacific Oceans.

26. Bali

27. He owned a milk bar and sandwich shop.

28. Joanne lived at the back of the shop.

29. **3 years old**

30. **Joanne's father read bedtime stories to Joanne.**

31. **He finished at 9 o'clock.**

32. **milk, malt, ice cream and chocolate flavouring**

33. **He called in for a chat.**

34. **He worked from 8 am in the morning until 9 pm at night.**

35. **The Taj Mahal** would be a good title for this passage.

36. **Shah Jahan** built the Taj Mahal.

37. It took **21** years to build.

38. This is **an exclamation**. The hint is the exclamation mark (!).

39. The Story of Apples. The correct order is:

   1 Seeds are planted in the ground and watered regularly.

   2 As the apple tree begins to grow, the plants are sprayed to keep the pests away.

   3 Flowers begin as tight buds. These are the buds of apple tree flowers.

   4 The apple blossoms open. Bees or other insects carry pollen from one flower to another. This is called pollination.

   5 The petals drop off the flower and the apple grows.

   6 When the apples are ripe they are picked and then packed into cartons.

   7 The fruit is taken to the market and sold.

See the Glossary on pages 148–151 for an explanation of grammar and punctuation terms.

CONVENTIONS OF LANGUAGE TEST 1 (pp. 91–96)

1. **is**

2. **?** Many of the errors that need to be corrected are punctuation errors. Some of them are hard to spot.

3. **'** Single or double quotation marks can be used, as long as they are the same before AND after the sentence or statement. They are both correct.

4. **Jack's**. Make sure you know how to use apostrophes to indicate possession — even adults make mistakes with them.

5. **I've**. This is an example where an apostrophe is used to indicate a contraction: *I have* → *I've*.

6. **see**

7. **are**

8. **come**

9. **lived**

10. **tamed**

11. **When**

12. **its**

13. **there**

14. **heaven.**

15. **for**

16. **they are**

17. **under the ground.**

18. **boy**. *Boy* is a noun. A noun is a person, place or thing.

19. **white**. An adjective describes. The word *white* describes the *shirt*.

20. **the girls**. A pronoun is a word in place of a noun. In this case it has to also be plural (more than one).

21. **I would**

22. **It is a proper noun.**

23. **a verb.**

24. **think**

25. **kinder**

26. **poor**

27. **kind**

28. **most**

29. **sold**

30. **moon**

31. **fast**

32. **class**

33. **football**

34. **children**

35. **mother**

36. **even**

37. wooden
38. sugar
39. until
40. better
41. birthday
42. meal
43. surprise
44. home
45. too
46. explore
47. many
48. quiet
49. beach
50. find

CONVENTIONS OF LANGUAGE
TEST 2 (pp. 99–104)

1. **Hannah**
2. **day.** Notice that you have to include the word and the full stop.
3. **was**
4. **'Quiet**
5. **stood**
6. **pen**. *Pen* is a noun because it is the name of a thing.
7. **little**. The adjective *little* describes the noun *cousin*.
8. **her**. This is a pronoun because *her* stands for *Jan*. A pronoun stands for a noun.
9. **from an egg**
10. **The female butterfly, which was a beautiful mixture of colours, laid her eggs under a leaf and …** There are commas around the phrase. Get someone to show you this if it isn't clear to you. We have underlined them so that they are easier for you to see.
11. **"The caterpillar will attach itself to a nearby branch and begin spinning its cocoon."** Remember to use speech marks (" and ") or inverted commas when people are speaking or for what they have said.
12. **After a little while you and I will see …** Both *you will see* and *I will see* and the two combined also *will see*.
13. **Most**
14. **Sentences 4 and 5**
15. **Everest**
16. **compare**
17. **verb**
18. **I will be counting.**
19. **Its coat was rough and covered in mud.**
20. **We are headed to Adelaide.**
21. **If**
22. **The sign was glued to a wall.**
23. **looked**
24. **"Here pony," said Hannah.**
25. **he will go**
26. **door**
27. **old**
28. **pink**
29. **mind**
30. **lost**
31. **soon**
32. **plant**
33. **bath**
34. **last**
35. **brother**
36. **great**
37. **many**
38. **people**
39. **money**
40. **climb**
41. **near**
42. **lose**
43. **no**
44. **pretty**
45. **their**
46. **Please**
47. **have**
48. **feet**
49. **pause**
50. **rowed**

CONVENTIONS OF LANGUAGE TEST 3 (pp. 107–111)

1. **They.** Start the sentence with a capital letter. They were very angry.
2. **is.** The subject of the verb (*He*) is singular and so needs a singular verb.
3. **Perth.** Perth is the name of a place and a proper noun so should begin with a capital letter.
4. **to.** He listened to each student say their speech.
5. **I.** The personal pronoun *I* is part of the subject of the sentence and so needs to be in the subject form.
6. Nicholas and Mary-Ellen **are** cousins.
7. Anthony **and** John are brothers.
8. Angelena used to live at **17 Edward Avenue**.
9. John's school was **Waverley College at Bondi**.
10. **bus**. This word is a noun because it is the name of a thing.
11. **funny**. The adjective *funny* describes the *movie*.
12. **we**. The pronoun *we* is in place of a noun.
13. **and**
14. **for**
15. **We**
16. **,** (comma)
17. **are**
18. **from**
19. **things**
20. **is**
21. **are**
22. **which**
23. **of**
24. **means**
25. **you've**
26. **floor**
27. **find**
28. **book**
29. **tree**
30. **gold**
31. **path**
32. **past**
33. **boat**
34. **pretty**
35. **father**
36. **finger**
37. **could**
38. **today**
39. **begin**
40. **visit**
41. **some**
42. **smooth**
43. **water**
44. **tails**
45. **bigger**
46. **found**
47. **countries**. When a word ends in a consonant before *y*, the plural is formed by changing the *y* into *ies*.
48. **along**
49. **search**
50. **bury**

CONVENTIONS OF LANGUAGE TEST 4 (pp. 114–119)

1. **knew**
2. **first**
3. **Gerry's**
4. **It**
5. **Miss Good**
6. **Ted's**
7. **to**
8. **She**
9. **door.** This is a noun because it is a thing.
10. **early.** *Early* is an adjective because it describes the noun *bus*.

11. **my friends.** This is the only answer option that can replace the third-person plural pronoun *they*. The other answer options are incorrect: *my coach* is singular, while *Nicholas and I* and *Sam and me* replace the first-person plural pronoun *we*.

12. **into**

13. **and**

14. **to**

15. **off**

16. The early **A**ustralian sports were a mixture of those from **E**ngland and **I**reland. (We have underlined the corrections and also highlighted them in bold to make them easier to see.)

17. Australia plays all sports. Australia is a world leader in swimming.

18. Sport is something to be enjoyed by everyone. It is fun and enjoyable.

19. "Is it true that Australia has taken part in every Olympics?" asked Jim.

20. He said, "Sport helps keep you fit and relaxed. It provides enjoyment."

21. **are eating** (Nick and Leo are eating fish for lunch.)

22. **Anthony's** (Jim is Anthony's father.)

23. **,** (Place a comma after teacher, that is: Max, who is a teacher, used to live in Maroubra.)

24. **better** (John said that his sore leg is better.)

25. **tallest** (Peter is the tallest in the family.)

26. **sat**

27. **look**

28. **home**

29. **land**

30. **hold**

31. **felt**

32. **grass**

33. **road**

34. **behind**

35. **children**

36. **sister**

37. **should**

38. **crowd**

39. **shake**

40. **thinking**

41. **jungle**

42. **under**

43. **depend**

44. **provide**

45. **spreading**

46. **inhabitants.** When spelling multisyllable words it is helpful to say them slowly so that you can hear all the parts clearly.

47. **tiny**

48. **magnifying**

49. **naked**

50. **know**

Notes

Notes

SPELLING WORDS FOR CONVENTIONS OF LANGUAGE TESTS

To the teacher or parent

First read and say the word slowly and clearly. Then read the sentence with the word in it. Then repeat the word again.

If the student is not sure, then ask them to guess. It is okay to skip a word if it is not known.

Spelling words for Conventions of Language Test 1

Word	Example
26. poor	The poor girl had no money.
27. kind	It is important to be kind to others.
28. most	I like to read most of the time.
29. sold	The house was sold.
30. moon	It is a bright yellow moon.
31. fast	Come as fast as you can.
32. class	The class is busy working.
33. football	They play football on the weekend.
34. children	Help the children to safety.
35. mother	My mother always cares for me.
36. even	Even the adults enjoyed the party.
37. wooden	This is a wooden toy car.
38. sugar	Sugar and spice and everything nice
39. until	Wait until I call you.
40. better	I better do it straight away.

Spelling words for Conventions of Language Test 2

Word	Example
26. door	The door is open.
27. old	I am an old man.
28. pink	Pink is a colour.
29. mind	Do you mind if I sit?
30. lost	He lost his way.
31. soon	Come as soon as you can.
32. plant	The plant grew quickly.
33. bath	The bath is filled with water.
34. last	Their horse came last in the race.
35. brother	His brother is a kind man.
36. great	I think this music is great.
37. many	Many happy returns!
38. people	The people watched the show.
39. money	How much money do we need?
40. climb	He will climb the mountain.

SPELLING WORDS FOR CONVENTIONS OF LANGUAGE TESTS

To the teacher or parent

First read and say the word slowly and clearly. Then read the sentence with the word in it. Then repeat the word again.

If the student is not sure, then ask them to guess. It is okay to skip a word if it is not known.

Spelling words for Conventions of Language Test 3

Word	Example
26. floor	She sat on the floor.
27. find	I will find a way.
28. book	You cannot judge a book by its cover.
29. tree	The tree is very large.
30. gold	Gold is a precious metal.
31. path	The path to the shed was overgrown with bushes.
32. past	They drove past the school.
33. boat	There is a small boat in the harbour.
34. pretty	The flowers in the vase were pretty.
35. father	My father is my friend.
36. finger	The little finger on his hand was injured.
37. could	Could we do this a better way?
38. today	Today is the first day of the competition.
39. begin	I shall begin my work shortly.
40. visit	Come and visit me as soon as you can.

Spelling words for Conventions of Language Test 4

Word	Example
26. sat	The cat sat on the mat.
27. look	I will look at the stars.
28. home	There is no place like home.
29. land	The pilot will land the aircraft.
30. hold	Hold on tight!
31. felt	The poor girl felt sad.
32. grass	You may walk on the grass.
33. road	The road was long and winding.
34. behind	They were just behind the leader.
35. children	The children enjoyed themselves at the party.
36. sister	My sister is kind.
37. should	I should help others in need.
38. crowd	The crowd applauded the pianist.
39. shake	Shake the toy and then watch it move.
40. thinking	There is much thinking to be done.